Sunset

ROSES

BY PHILIP EDINGER AND THE EDITORS OF SUNSET BOOKS

SUNSET BOOKS INC. · MENLO PARK, CALIFORNIA

ALWAYS ROSES

In 1955, Sunset published *How to Grow Roses*, a pioneering soft-cover book designed for the home gardener. Its 80 pages presented the essentials of rose growing, along with descriptions of popular roses of the era (chiefly hybrid teas). In the more than four decades since, four new editions have appeared—each longer than the original volume by 16 pages, each updated to keep abreast of changes in gardening styles and to include advances in rose culture and profiles of new varieties.

This sixth edition is *Sunset's* latest testament to the public's love affair with the rose (and, at 128 pages, our longest one as well). Like its predecessors, it offers advice on all aspects of growing roses and describes a wide array of favorites

Gloire des Mousseaux

among the ever-popular hybrid tea class. In tune with the growing interest in more and varied roses, however, we also present a rich assortment of roses in many other classes, from historic treasures to more recent beauties. You'll encounter knee-high miniatures, tree-tall climbers, and just about everything in between. Read on to plan a truly rosy future.

Throughout the years, experts from around the country (now a lengthy "who's who" of rosarians) have generously shared their knowledge with us, helping ensure that the information we provide is accurate and up to date. We are grateful to Virginia Hopper of Branscomb, California for her valuable suggestions on the current edition.

SUNSET BOOKS INC.

Director, Sales and Marketing: Richard A. Smeby
Editorial Director: Bob Doyle
Production Director: Lory Day
Art Director: Vasken Guiragossian

Staff for this book:

Managing Editor: Suzanne Normand Eyre
Copy Editor and Indexer: Rebecca LaBrum
Photo Researcher: Tishana Peebles
Production Coordinator: Patricia S. Williams
Proofreader: Marianne Lipanovich

Art Director: Alice Rogers
Page Layouts: Phippen Design Group
Illustrator: Lois Lovejoy
Computer Production: Fog Press

Cover: 'Graham Thomas'. Photography by David McDonald.
Border photograph (*Rosa banksiae* 'Lutea') by Saxon Holt.

PHOTOGRAPHERS:

All-America Rose Selections: 51 top left; **Art Resource:** 7 top right, 8 left; **Scott Atkinson:** 3 top left, 4, 10 left, 53, 83 top left, 98, 101; **Max E. Badgley:** 110 top left 1; **Bill Beatty/Visuals Unlimited:** 110 top right 1; **R. S. Byther:** 110 top right 3 and bottom left 2; **David Cavagnaro:** 2, 18 bottom left, 22 bottom, 27 top right, 29 bottom left, 32 bottom right, 59 bottom right, 65 top; **Glenn Christiansen:** 60 top; **Sharon J. Collman:** 110 bottom right 1; **Ken Conway:** 110 bottom left 1; **Crandall & Crandall:** 110 top left 3; **J. D. Cunningham/Visuals Unlimited:** 110 bottom left 3; **Claire Curran:** 49 upper middle, 62 middle right, 64 top right, 65 bottom right, 70 bottom left, 81 bottom; **Arnaud Descat/M.A.P.:** 3 top right, lower middle left, 14, 72, 80 bottom right; **Alan and Linda Detrick:** 49 lower middle, 87 top right, bottom, 88 bottom left; **Ken Druse:** 60 bottom left, 61 middle right, 75 top right, 77 middle left, 79 middle right, bottom left, 126; **Philip Edinger:** 30 top right, bottom left, 35 bottom left, top right, 37 top left, top right; **Derek Fell:** 3 bottom right, 16 bottom right, 17 top right, bottom, 25 bottom left, 43 top right, 44 bottom left, 46 top left, 50 top right, 59 bottom left, 61 top left, middle left, 62 bottom left, 66 middle center, 67 top left, 68 bottom center, 70 top left, middle right, 78 top, 80 bottom left, 83 bottom right, 84, 88 middle left, 89 top right, middle right, 90 bottom, 95 top left, 122; **William E. Ferguson:** 110 bottom right 2; **Robert Fried:** 6 middle and bottom; **Christopher Gardner:** 99 top left; **David Goldberg:** 94 bottom; **William A. Grant:** 10 right, 46 bottom left, 91 bottom right; **Lynne Harrison:** 3 middle right, 6 top, 17 top left, 20 middle, bottom left, 25 top left, 50 middle, 54, 58 middle left, 61 top right, 62 middle left, 78 bottom, 79 top right, middle left, 81 top, back cover top left; **Philip Harvey:** 100; **Saxon Holt:** 1, 3 bottom left, 7 top left, 8 bottom right, 11, 16 top, 18 middle, 20 top right, 21, 22 middle, 25 bottom right, 26 left, 27 bottom, 28, 30 top left, 30 bottom right, 33 top left, bottom left, bottom right, 35 middle, 36 bottom, 37 bottom left, 38, 39 left, 43 bottom left, 49 bottom, 57, 58 top right, 62 bottom right, 65 middle, 66 middle left, 68 top left, 69 bottom right, 70 middle left, 71, 76 top, bottom left, 77 top, 80 top, 82 top, 88 top center, middle right, 89 bottom, 91 top right, 92, 125, back cover bottom; **Erich Lessing/Art Resource:** 7 bottom right, 9; **Allan Mandell:** 3 upper middle left, 40, 47 top right, bottom right, 63, 68 top center, 95 bottom; **Charles Mann:** 8 bottom left, 17 middle, 30 middle, 31, 33 top right, 34, 94 top, 96 top; **Ells Marugg:** 44 bottom center, 47 left, 49 top, 50 top left, 58 bottom left, 67 top right, 86 bottom left, 89 top left, middle left, middle center, 90 middle right; **David McDonald/PhotoGarden:** 44 top left, 58 top left, bottom right, 59 top left, 66 bottom right, 77 middle right; **Jack McDowell:** 44 bottom center, 48 top left; **N. and P. Mioulane/M.A.P.:** 75 top left; **Clive Nichols/M.A.P.:** 75 bottom; **Jerry Pavia:** 8 top right, 12, 16 bottom left, 20 top left, 23 top, 32 top, 35 upper middle left, 36 top, 43 middle right, 45 top left, 46 top right, 47 middle right, 51 middle left, middle right, 52 top, 56, 62 top left, 64 top left, 66 top right, 67 bottom left, 68 bottom left, right, 69 middle, 75 middle, 76 middle, bottom right, 78 middle, 83 top right, 86 bottom right, 87 top left, 88 top right, 90 top right, 96 bottom, 124; **Joanne Pavia:** 45 top left, 51 bottom right, 52 upper middle right, bottom; **Norman A. Plate:** 52 lower middle, 69 top left, 99 top right, bottom right, 103 left, 104, 105, 107, 108, 109, 112, 119, 120, 121; **James H. Robinson:** 110 top left 2; **Susan Roth:** 18 top left, top right, 19 bottom, 20 bottom right, 29 bottom right, 25 top right, 27 top left, 43 top left, 60 bottom right, 77 bottom, 95 top right, back cover top right; **Kjell Sandved/Visuals Unlimited:** 110 top right 2; **Sequoia Nursery:** 91 bottom left; **K. Bryan Swezey:** 67 bottom right, 106 middle, 115; **Anthony Tesselaar:** 62 top right; **Michael S. Thompson:** 18 bottom right, 19 top, 22 top, 23 top, 26 right, 29 top right, middle right, bottom right, 32 bottom left, 39 bottom left, top, 45 bottom right, 48 bottom, 50 bottom, 59 middle left, middle right, 61 bottom left, bottom right, 64 middle left, middle right, 65 bottom left, 66 middle right, 68 top right, 69 top right, bottom right, 70 top right, bottom right, 79 bottom right, 90 middle left, 96 top right, 97, 103 right, 116; **Darrow M. Watt:** 106 top; **Ron West:** 110 bottom right 1; **Tom Wyatt:** 24, 35 lower middle right, 42, 43 middle right, 48 top center, top right, 52 upper middle left, 58 middle left, 59 top right, 64 bottom right, 82 bottom, 86 top, bottom center, 106 bottom right.

CONTENTS

From spring into autumn, you see roses everywhere. Beautiful in form, blooming in a rainbow of colors, often enticingly fragrant, they're mainstays of public and private gardens.

INTRODUCING THE
QUEEN

Few would argue that they deserve the name "queen of flowers." The surprise is that this regal title was bestowed by the Greek poet Sappho over 2,500 years ago, when all to be had were wild roses—blooms of a decidedly demure demeanor. Even those simple blossoms, it seems, had a loveliness and presence that set them apart.

In the classical Mediterranean world, Sappho was the first to elevate the rose to royal status, but far from the first to take written note of it. Roses are mentioned in the Iliad and Odyssey of Homer; four centuries later—in the 5th century B.C.—the historian Herodotus remarked on King Midas's rose garden in Phrygia. A century after that, Theophrastus recorded botanical descriptions of contemporary roses, noting that the flowers were grown in Egypt as well as in Greece. At about the same time—but thousands of miles to the east—Confucius commented on extensive rose plantings in the Peking Imperial Gardens.

Ancient art provides yet more evidence of our long-standing romance with the rose. Asian coins minted as far back as 4,000 B.C. bear rose motifs; single rose blossoms

Introduced in 1843, the Bourbon rose 'Souvenir de la Malmaison' (page 33) commemorates the early-19th-century rose garden established by France's Empress Josephine.

appear in Cretan frescoes dating to 1,600 B.C.; rose-inspired architectural decorations have been discovered in Assyrian and Babylonian ruins. Chaplets found adorning Egyptian mummies contain desiccated rose blossoms that may be from *Rosa × richardii,* a plant still cultivated today—more often under the common names "St. John's rose" or "rose of the tombs."

In the following pages, we offer a brief history of the rose, tracing the ways the modest flowers beloved of Sappho have led to the glorious and varied blooms that grace today's gardens.

WHEN IN ROME...

By the time the Roman Empire replaced Greece as the dominant civilization in the Mediterranean basin, roses were already an integral part of Roman society. The flowers decorated parties, weddings, and funerals; on festival days and other important occasions, statues and monuments were wreathed in roses, and the streets were strewn with their petals. Rose-draped warriors departed for battle with rose-adorned shields and chariots. Wealthy Romans could bathe in rose water, wear rose garlands, eat confections made from rose petals, and sip rose wine. When ill, they could take medicines prepared from rose petals, seeds, or hips (given the vitamin C content of rose hips, some of these potions may have been genuinely beneficial). To support such widespread demand, a thriving rose-growing industry developed, much of it located in Egypt (then a Roman colony), where winters were mild.

While upper-class Romans reveled in the sensual delights that roses could provide, the plants attracted scholarly attention as well: Pliny's first-century *Natural History* records the different types, colors, and growth habits of the roses then in cultivation.

EXALTATION OF ROSES

The Roman Empire was ultimately to collapse of its own bureaucratic weight, geographic extension, and corruption, but not before its emperors had officially embraced a new religion: Christianity. The disintegration of the empire left millions of now-Christian Romans scattered from England to North Africa to the Black Sea— a population with a rose-infused past. It was not surprising, then, that the flowers eventually took on religious significance. Roses became a symbol for survivors of religious persecution; a white rose often represented the Immaculate Conception of the Virgin Mary. The word "rosary," originally meaning simply "rose garden," later came to refer to the series of prayers related to the life of Christ and the Virgin. The rose's role in Christian imagery is perhaps most magnificently expressed, however, in the stained glass "rose windows" of medieval cathedrals—intricately fashioned circular windows with petal-like panels radiating from the center.

Of course, roses still had a place in secular life and symbolism. From the earliest days of chivalry, they were a favored motif in heraldry (a legacy, perhaps, of the rose-bedecked Roman shields and chariots). Beginning with Edward I in 1272, several English monarchs took the rose as a royal badge. Such usage gave the Wars of the Roses their name: the conflict involved the houses of York and Lancaster, whose emblems were a white and a red rose, respectively.

Ironically, perhaps, certain practical Roman uses of the rose were kept alive only by religion. In hundreds of Christian monasteries scattered over western Europe, rose plants were cultivated for medicine, for perfume, and perhaps even for Communion wine.

TOP: *Rosa × richardii,* the "rose of the tombs"
BOTTOM: Rose windows from the cathedral at Chartres

Old Blush (China)

SETTING THE STAGE

In the Renaissance of western Europe, science and the arts flourished as they had not done since the classical civilizations of over a thousand years earlier. In art, wordly themes began to appear more frequently; Renaissance canvases often celebrated daily life, ordinary people, landscapes—and flowers. Noteworthy are countless Flemish and Dutch floral still-lifes: their mixed bouquets include realistic portraits of roses, blossoms of a style and fullness that identify them as members of old rose classes that survive to this day.

In the Renaissance, plants came to be cultivated for beauty as much as for utility, and new and different kinds were sought out and brought into cultivation. These trends continued in subsequent centuries, setting the stage for the development of the roses we know today. Thus, trade between western Europe and the exotic East—Japan, China, and India—involved not only goods such as spices and fabrics; living plants were imported as well, thanks to burgeoning scientific curiosity and a growing upper class with an interest in magnificent gardens. Throughout the 17th and 18th centuries, the East India Companies of England, France, and Holland funneled unfamiliar plants to private collectors and botanical gardens across Europe. Among the new arrivals were four roses destined to revolutionize the garden rose as it was then known.

Although there is some dispute over exactly when and where each of these four "China roses" made its European debut, we do know that the first two, 'Parson's Pink China' (now known as 'Old Blush') and 'Slater's Crimson China', were established in England by about 1792. Both these plants were garden selections of *Rosa chinensis* that had been grown by the Chinese for centuries. Their clustered, smallish flowers were a far cry from the opulent European roses of the time, but they had one significant trait in their favor: they flowered repeatedly from spring until stopped by frost.

Some years later, in the early to mid-1800s, two other significant Asian imports reached Europe: 'Hume's Blush Tea-scented China' and 'Park's Yellow Tea-scented China'. The ancestors of the tea rose class (see pages 36–37), these plants would be recognized today as the first to resemble the familiar modern hybrid teas.

TOP: *Empress Josephine Seated at Malmaison* by François Gérard
BOTTOM: *Roses in a Blue Vase* by the 17th-century
Flemish artist Jan Bruegel the Elder

The China roses' first appearance on the European scene was closely followed by a second event of great consequence for rose history: the ascension of Napoleon I and his empress, Josephine, to the throne of France. The daughter of a wealthy planter from the Caribbean island of Martinique, Josephine loved flowers in general and roses in particular, and she determined to use her vast financial resources to collect and maintain all the roses then known in the western world. Begun in 1804, her collection at Malmaison, the imperial chateau, reached its zenith 10 years later, when it contained about 250 different rose species and varieties.

To preserve her treasured collection for posterity, the Empress summoned a group of artists to Malmaison, among them Pierre-Joseph Redouté, the "Raphael of the flowers." Accompanied with botanical descriptions by Claude-Antoine Thory, Redouté's watercolors were gathered in a three-volume collection, *Les Roses*, a work still unsurpassed in artistic detail and beauty.

TOP: Empress Josephine (hybrid gallica)
BOTTOM LEFT: *Rosa × damascena* (damask)
BOTTOM RIGHT: Apothecary's Rose (gallica)

So renowned and respected was Josephine's endeavor that it transcended even international animosities. The British, then at war with France, permitted plants found on captured French ships to be sent on to Malmaison. And when the Napoleonic Wars ended in 1815, the victorious British troops were ordered to protect the Malmaison garden from harm.

Sadly, without royal patronage to provide inspiration and maintenance, the garden soon fell into disrepair. But its greater mission had been accomplished.

Rosa × centifolia 'Bullata' by Pierre-Joseph Redouté

Reaching its peak at a time when European horticultural horizons were rapidly expanding, the Malmaison garden opened the eyes of botanists, gardeners, and future rose growers. It spawned a French rose industry that developed and propagated roses for an ever-expanding market of wealthy and emerging middle-class landowners. The Malmaison roses furnished both inspiration and breeding material, putting rose evolution on a fast track toward the roses we now think of as modern.

CLASSIFICATION OF ROSES

The roses at Malmaison also encouraged serious efforts at botanical classification. Confronted by an unprecedented grouping of similar yet differing plants, botanists and horticulturists of the day recognized certain individuals as species, then organized the others into several distinct classes (described below), based on appearance and presumed ancestry. Collectively, these are now known as old European roses; save for 'Autumn Damask', all flower only in late spring or early summer.

GALLICA ROSES. Over half of the Malmaison collection was made up of gallica roses—variants (and in some cases hybrids) of *Rosa gallica*. Also called "French rose," the species grows wild in western Europe; in nature, it bears pink to light red, highly fragrant blossoms on compact, upright plants.

DAMASK ROSES have an obscure history that stretches back thousands of years; contemporary research suggests that *Rosa gallica, R. phoenicia,* and *R. moschata* (the musk rose) may all figure in the group's ancestry. Summer-flowering *R. × damascena,* possibly native to Asia Minor, seems to have been spread through the Mediterranean basin by Phoenician traders or Greek colonists, if not by the Egyptians. Legend has it that the Crusaders later brought the rose from the Holy Land to Europe; the specific name *damascena* refers to Damascus, Syria. The one repeat-flowering rose known to the ancient world was a damask, the plant the Romans named "rose of Paestum" (or of Cyrinae or Carthage); its likeness appears on frescoes in Pompeii. Long afterward, Spanish missionaries brought the same rose to North America, where it was called "rose of Castile." Botanically known as *R. × damascena* 'Bifera' ('Semperflorens'), it has also been given the garden name 'Autumn Damask'. Josephine's collection contained this and seven other damask roses.

ALBA ROSES are an ancient group of natural hybrids of complex ancestry. Their flowers are white (as the name implies) or pink, carried on tall, shrubby to semiclimbing plants. Nine albas grew at Malmaison.

CENTIFOLIA ROSES constituted about one-eighth of the collection at Malmaison. These are the full, lush, typically pink or white roses beloved of Dutch and Flemish painters; many are intensely fragrant. The name literally means "hundred-leafed," a reference to the countless petals packed into each blossom. Like the albas, the centifolias are a hybrid group—deriving, in fact, from a mix of alba and damask. Many of the oldest varieties are simply sports of the original *Rosa × centifolia* or of another sport; the most radical departures from the original are the moss roses (see pages 28–29).

In the 1800s, rose breeding proceeded at a frenzied pace. Growers continued to work with the Malmaison roses, raising new varieties that fit into the classes just described. But they were active on other fronts as well. The repeat-flowering Asian imports excited great interest, and growers in the mild-winter parts of France, in particular, vastly expanded the number of varieties in two new classes (Chinas and teas) derived strictly from Asian roses. In addition, breeders began raising hybrids—first naturally occurring hybrids, then deliberate crosses—between old European roses and Asian ones, creating yet more classes with plant and flower characteristics of both parents and, typically, some repeat bloom. The six rose classes described below, together with the old European roses, are known collectively as old garden roses.

CHINA ROSES' capacity for near-constant bloom inspired growers to plant countless seeds from the two original representatives and encouraged importation of additional plants and seeds from China and India. The net result was a sizable group of virtually everblooming plants producing small clusters of modest-sized pink, red, or white blossoms on bushy, twiggy plants of moderate stature.

PORTLAND ROSES, the first of which appeared around 1800, were the first hybrids between China roses, especially 'Slater's Crimson China', with old European types (particularly 'Autumn Damask'). These are stocky plants combining the floral character and colors of the European parent with the repeat-flowering ability of the China ancestor.

BOURBON ROSES arose by happy accident on the Île de Bourbon (now Réunion) in the Indian Ocean off Madagascar. Where fields were bordered by hedges of different roses, the appearance of hybrids was inevitable—and one of these, a cross between 'Old Blush' and 'Autumn Damask', was discovered in 1819 by a visiting French botanist. He sent seeds of the plant to the king's gardener in Paris, who raised a choice seedling which he christened 'Rosier de l'Île Bourbon': a repeat-flowering, semiclimbing plant with shiny leaves, purple-tinted canes, and semidouble pink blooms. Numerous hybrids were raised from this original Bourbon, the best of which retain the parent's foliage and plant characteristics as well as its capacity for repeat bloom. The old Bourbon-China hybrid 'Gloire des Rosomanes', one of the chief sources of red color in modern roses, persists in countless older gardens today. Ironically, it is not grown for its blooms; it was once used as an understock for modern roses.

NOISETTE ROSES are a New World contribution, contemporaneous with the establishment of Malmaison in France.

Roses in a Bowl (1882) by Henri Fantin-Latour

Blush Noisette (Noisette)

John Champneys, a rice planter in Charleston, South Carolina, raised a climbing hybrid between 'Old Blush' and *Rosa moschata* (the musk rose), calling it 'Champneys' Pink Cluster' for its large, profuse clusters of small spring-through-autumn blossoms. His neighbor, Philippe Noisette, sent seeds or seedlings of this rose (accounts vary) to his brother in France, who raised a shrubbier, darker pink rose from them. Introduced as 'Blush Noisette' in 1817, it was bred to produce a group of small-flowered, fairly hardy, shrubby semiclimbers with flowers in white through pink to crimson and purple.

TEA ROSES stem from the second two China roses imported from Asia: 'Hume's Blush Tea-scented China' (1810) and 'Park's Yellow Tea-scented China' (1824). Though "China" is part of each name, the two roses derive not only from *Rosa chinensis* but also from *R. gigantea*, a rampant, once-blooming, tender climber from the Himalayan foothills. Where these cold-intolerant plants would thrive—in the Caribbean islands and in mild-winter parts of France, Italy, Spain, and the United States, for example—they became the pre-eminent garden roses of their time. Inherently evergreen and ever-growing, resistant to foliage diseases, and virtually everblooming, they bear blossoms in white, melting pastels (cream, pink, yellow), and rosy red; many feature long, tapered buds and silken petals. Noisettes were crossed with these early teas (as well as with 'Park's Yellow Tea-scented China') to produce a number of tea-Noisette climbers, many of which may as well be climbing teas (sometimes with somewhat smaller blossoms). To modern roses, the teas bequeathed their flower form and overall refinement, as well as some of their lack of hardiness.

HYBRID PERPETUAL ROSES were the garden and cut-flower workhorses of the 19th century. The first varieties appeared around 1838, and the class dominated the rose industry until shortly after 1900. Though they do have repeat bloom in their makeup (their ancestry includes virtually all the classes that preceded them), labeling them "perpetual" was something of an overstatement: a massive spring show was followed by only scattered bloom (or a smaller autumn burst). The French called them *hybrides remontants* ("reblooming hybrids"), a more accurate appellation. Most bear large, lush, full-petaled flowers in colors ranging from white through all shades of pink and red to purple; husky, even rampant growth is the norm.

THE MODERN ERA

Though many rose lovers still treasure the old garden types, the majority of roses grown and sold today belong to the modern classes.

HYBRID TEA ROSES did not enter the scene with bells and whistles; they crept in imperceptibly, recognized only after the fact as roses of a type different from those that had come before. Just which rose was the first of the group is a subject of some controversy; by tradition, if not consensus, the honor falls to 'La France', putting the birth of the class in the year 1867.

La France (hybrid tea)

The original hybrid teas were the logical outcome of breeders' attempts to combine the robustness of a hybrid perpetual with the refinement of a tea rose. Their characteristics fell midway between those of the two parent types: they were more perpetual than the hybrid perpetuals but not as profusely blooming as the teas; their hardiness was variable but usually better than that of their tender tea parent. They had the color range of the hybrid perpetuals, with the addition of creamy yellow from the teas.

In 1900, however, an unusual hybrid was introduced that would dramatically broaden the color palette—and have serious consequences for plant health. After years of effort, Joseph Pernet succeeded in crossing the brilliant yellow 'Persian Yellow' (the double yellow form of *Rosa foetida,* the Austrian brier) with a purple-red hybrid perpetual. The result was 'Soleil d'Or' ("golden sun"), a repeat-flowering, reasonably hardy, yellow-orange bush rose. Though not a hybrid tea by appearance or ancestry, 'Soleil d'Or' did remarkable things when crossed with one. In two or three generations, hybrid teas appeared bearing blossoms in exciting new colors: vivid golden yellow, flame, copper, soft orange, and bicolors of yellow and almost any other color.

These exotic new hues came with a hidden price. Along with its vibrant color, the *R. foetida* parent passed along a tendency toward poorly formed blossoms and foliage which, though lustrous, was especially prone to disease. Intolerance of pruning was another legacy: if canes were cut back severely—by hard pruning or a harsh winter—the plants often died.

Soleil d'Or

For a number of years, these hybrid tea–'Soleil d'Or' crosses formed a separate subclass called Pernetianas. By the 1930s, however, they had been crossed so extensively with hybrid teas that distinctions between the two groups were slight to nonexistent. Today, the glorious Pernetiana colors have permeated all other modern rose classes; in many cases, varieties showing Pernetiana hues still have a definite resentment of pruning. Strange as it may seem, Pernetiana heritage is also responsible for most modern roses in shades of mauve, lavender, gray, tan, and brown.

POLYANTHA AND FLORIBUNDA ROSES are something of the modern equivalent of Noisettes. The earliest polyanthas, derived from the Japanese *Rosa multiflora* and various tea roses (and their relatives, including tea-Noisettes), appeared in France at about the time the first hybrid teas did. They were short, compact plants that flowered almost constantly, bearing full but rather formless, white or pink blooms about an inch across; the blossoms were carried in clusters so large they nearly obscured the foliage. Inevitably, the polyanthas were crossed with hybrid teas, yielding plants that bloomed as profusely as the polyanthas but had better-formed flowers in a wider range of colors. The Poulsen family of Denmark were pioneers in this line of breeding, developing roses hardy enough for the northern European climate, as free-flowering as the polyanthas yet with bigger, individually beautiful blossoms. It soon became clear that these new crosses needed a new designation, since their larger flowers and bulkier, bushier plants set them apart from their polyantha parents. Finally, in the 1940s, the term "floribunda" was coined.

Through repeated breeding with hybrid teas, floribundas have continued to evolve beyond the original semidouble types. Many of today's floribundas offer the best hybrid tea flower form and the full range of hybrid tea colors; in fact, some depart from hybrid teas only in their cluster-flowering habit.

GRANDIFLORA ROSES represent the near-total absorption of floribunda into hybrid tea. Like "floribunda," the name "grandiflora" was devised as a marketing label, but it is well chosen. Grandifloras usually are larger and more vigorous than the average hybrid tea; their flowers may be as large as those of hybrid teas, but they come in few-flowered clusters on fairly long stems.

MINIATURE ROSES have a long history. All the old European rose types (gallicas, damasks, albas, centifolias, even mosses) have corresponding miniature varieties—and all fell into disfavor with the introduction of the repeat-flowering miniature China rose *(Rosa chinensis minima)*. Its exact origin is cloudy, but the plants reached Europe shortly after 1800, apparently imported from Mauritius, an island in the Indian Ocean under British control.

Miniature roses have gone through two widely separated periods of development. The first spanned the years from about 1820 to 1850, coming to an end when the advent of the polyanthas eclipsed the popularity of miniature Chinas. The second wave of miniature rose breeding began around 1930, 10 years after an attractive miniature China was discovered growing profusely in windowboxes in two Swiss villages. Using this rose ('Rouletii') and the similar 19th-century China rose 'Pompon de Paris', hybridizers have developed a new race of miniatures from crosses with polyanthas, floribundas, and hybrid teas. These modern types vary in flower and plant size, but typically replicate current hybrid tea colors and, frequently, flower form. Crosses between miniatures and climbing derivatives of *R. wichuraiana* have produced a series of climbing and trailing miniatures; crosses with moss roses have yielded miniatures with mossy characteristics.

SHRUB ROSES constitute "everything else"—one reason why the name is not an entirely accurate description of the class. Adventurous breeders aiming for disease-resistant, vigorous plants that flower repeatedly, bear shapely blossoms, and withstand harsh winters with scant or no protection have produced an immensely varied, very useful, rapidly expanding group of flowering shrubs. Some, however, are more like small climbers than shrubs, while the truly lax-caned among them are actual ground covers. And in between is—well, everything else you can imagine. Nostalgia and reverence for the past are reflected in the English roses, repeat-flowering shrubs with blossoms of old European style and scent in the full range of hybrid tea colors. Midwestern and Canadian breeders are widening the range of tough-as-nails plants that can stand up to northern and prairie winters. Unusual or untried species have been added to the melting pot; hybrids with a species that may not even be a rose *(Hulthemia—* or *Rosa—persica)* are pointing the way to who knows where. These catch-all roses are truly the future—and they are *now!*

THE EVOLUTION OF ROSES

The charts on these two pages outline the development of the major rose classes. The spring-flowering old European roses appear below. The facing page covers the descendants of the China roses, repeat-blooming classes that include the types most widely grown today. The ancestries sketched here are general. The original Bourbon rose, for example, did arise from a cross of 'Old Blush' with 'Autumn Damask', but later Bourbons represent a variety of combinations departing from the original fifty-fifty percentage (though they do ultimately stem from the first two parents).

Origins of Old European Roses

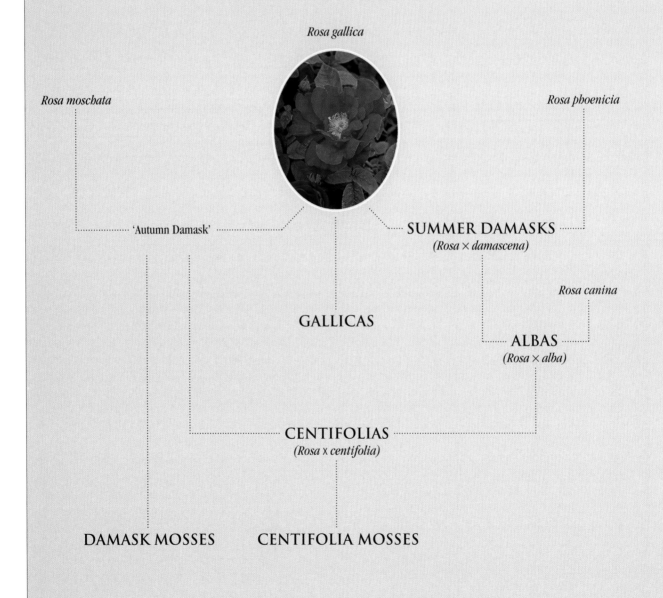

Rosa gallica

Rosa moschata

Rosa phoenicia

'Autumn Damask'

SUMMER DAMASKS
(Rosa × damascena)

Rosa canina

GALLICAS

ALBAS
(Rosa × alba)

CENTIFOLIAS
(Rosa × centifolia)

DAMASK MOSSES   CENTIFOLIA MOSSES

Development of Modern Roses

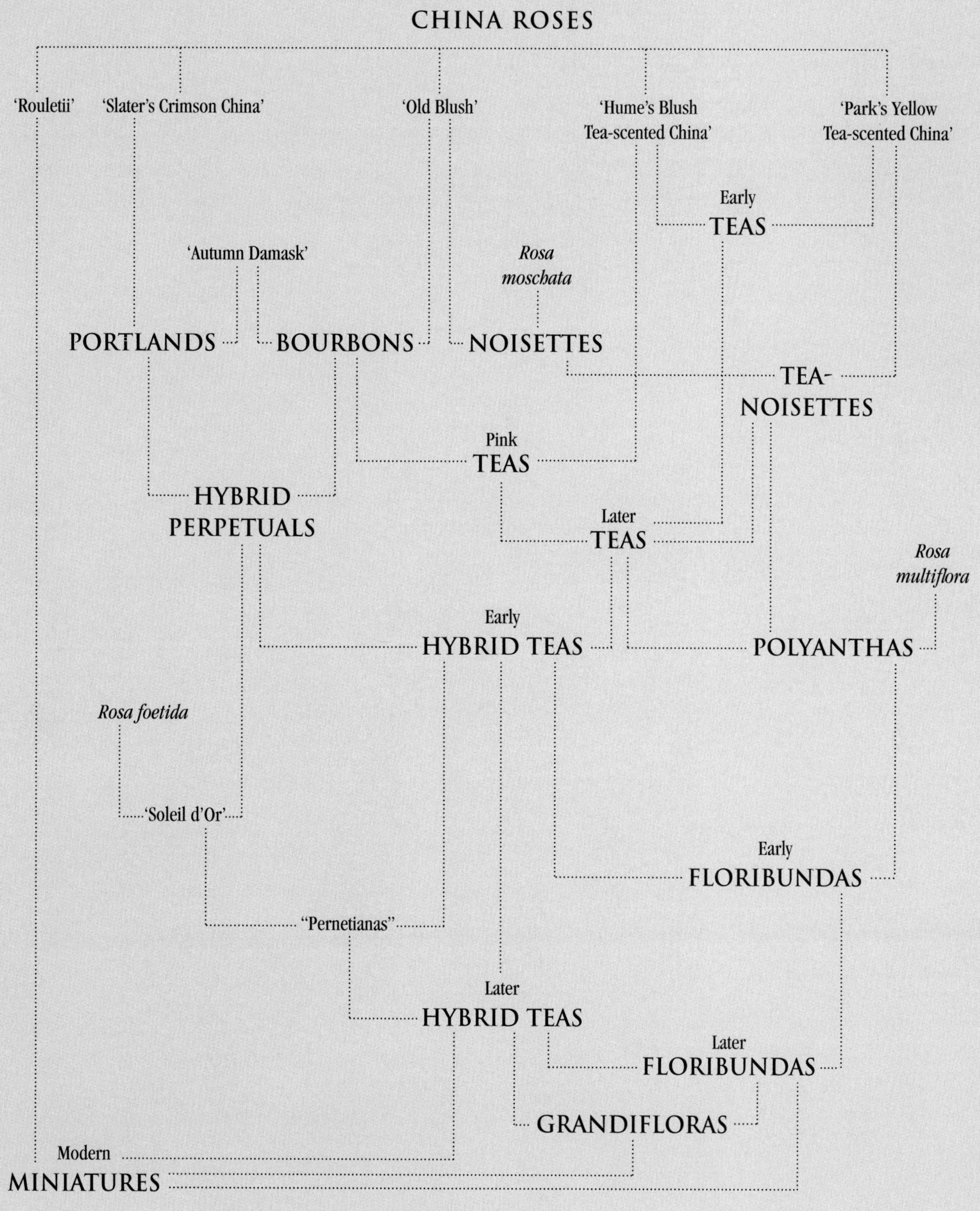

CHINA ROSES

'Rouletii' 'Slater's Crimson China' 'Old Blush' 'Hume's Blush Tea-scented China' 'Park's Yellow Tea-scented China'

Early TEAS

'Autumn Damask' *Rosa moschata*

PORTLANDS BOURBONS NOISETTES

TEA-NOISETTES

Pink TEAS

HYBRID PERPETUALS

Later TEAS

Rosa multiflora

Early HYBRID TEAS POLYANTHAS

Rosa foetida

'Soleil d'Or'

Early FLORIBUNDAS

"Pernetianas"

Later HYBRID TEAS

Later FLORIBUNDAS

GRANDIFLORAS

Modern MINIATURES

The evolutionary path leading to today's roses is a road that can still be walked by inquiring gardeners. The history of roses is alive, in bloom—and available from specialty growers.

Yesterday's
ROSES

Whether you fancy the simplicity of a species rose or the lush opulence of a centifolia, you'll find not merely a few examples of each kind, but entire selections from which to choose. And what a selection it is: 'Rose du Roi', 'Communis', 'Robert le Diable', 'Celestial', 'Austrian Copper', 'American Beauty', 'Maiden's Blush', 'Old Blush', 'Variegata di Bologna', 'Pompon de Bourgogne', 'Reine Victoria', 'Königin von Däne-mark', and a host of baronesses, duchesses, and countesses, with the occasional general, maréchal, or cardinal along the way. The richness of their names alone makes these historic roses worth cherishing.

In the 24 pages that follow, we discuss the historic rose classes presented in Chapter 1. From species roses to hybrid perpetuals, you'll meet the actual roses representing the groups that preceded today's familiar hybrid teas—and best of all, you can also meet them in your own garden.

Many old European roses, such as this centifolia ('Fantin-Latour', page 26), can become opulent flowering shrubs if given light pruning and plenty of water and fertilizer.

ROSE SPECIES

All rose development ultimately started with rose species—"wild roses," as they are commonly called. And though the changes wrought by hybridization (intended and natural) are indeed marvelous, the modest wild-rose charm still beguiles. The 15 species described here exemplify the geographic range of wild roses—from northern to near-tropical latitudes, from temperate lands with ample rain to regions of great aridity. Some are climbers, others are bushes—but all are worthy garden ornaments wherever their natural growth habits can be accommodated.

With a few exceptions (noted below), most will survive lows of at least −20°F/−29°C without significant protection. Only a few succeed in the heat and humidity of the Gulf Coast, Florida, and deep Southeast: Rosa banksiae, R. laevigata, R. moschata, *and* R. roxburghii. *Except as noted, all flower only in spring.*

ROSA BANKSIAE. Banksia rose

White or yellow. Western and central China. Where winter temperatures remain above 0°F/−18°C, these rampant climbers are smothered in bloom in early spring. Carried in pendent clusters, the 1-inch flowers are white or yellow; there are single and double forms of each color, but only the double-flowered versions are generally available. 'Lutea' (Lady Banks' rose) has primrose yellow, unscented blossoms; *R. banksiae banksiae* (usually sold as 'Alba Plena' or 'White Banksia') bears pure white flowers with the scent of violets. Stems are thornless in the double forms (single-flowered plants are thorny), bearing diseaseproof, aphid-resistant leaves composed of three to five narrow, leathery leaflets. Foliage is virtually evergreen in all but coldest areas of the plants' range.

ROSA CANINA. Dog rose, dog brier

White or pink. Europe, southwest Asia, northwest Africa. A familiar component of England's hedgerows, this species is well known to British gardeners for another reason too—for generations, it has provided the suckering under-stock onto which their garden roses are budded. Freed from its hedgerow and understock roles, it forms a bushy, arching shrub 8 to 15 feet tall, bearing single, 1- to 2-inch

TOP: *Rosa banksiae*
BOTTOM LEFT: *Rosa canina* (hips)
BOTTOM RIGHT: *Rosa canina*

blossoms individually or in small clusters. Flower color ranges from white to pale pink; oval, orange-red hips make an effective show in early autumn.

ROSA EGLANTERIA *(R. rubiginosa)*. Sweet brier, eglantine

Pink. Europe, western Asia, north Africa. This rose, the eglantine of Shakespeare, has a special appeal: both flowers and foliage have a green-apple fragrance (most pronounced in damp weather). Vigorous bushes with arching canes reach 8 to 12 feet; the dense, dark green foliage provides a backdrop for single pink flowers about 1½ inches wide. Oval, red to orange hips are decorative in autumn. Given an annual trimming, sweet brier can be used as a hedge.

ROSA FOETIDA. Austrian brier

Yellow; orange and yellow. Western Asia. Few spring bloomers put on a brighter show than this flashy rose and its variants. Slender, prickly canes form an upright to arching plant covered in dark green leaves—but the foliage is scarcely visible when mid- to late spring brings a shower of 2- to 3-inch, single blossoms in brilliant yellow. Most widely grown is *R. f.* 'Bicolor' (commonly called 'Austrian Copper'). Its blooms are a gypsyesque blaze of coppery orange petals with yellow backs; you'll often see bushes in which some canes have reverted to the pure yellow of the basic species. 'Persiana', also known as 'Persian Yellow', has golden blossoms that are fully double. *R. foetida* and its forms do best in dry-summer regions; they are susceptible to several foliage diseases.

ROSA GLAUCA (R. rubrifolia)

Pink. Mountains of central and southern Europe. This truly deserves a descriptive common name: it is the one species grown for its decorative foliage, which combines gray green and coppery purple. Arching, sparsely-thorned canes form a 6- to 9-foot bush studded with small, dark pink, single blossoms in spring. Small, oval hips turn red in autumn.

ROSA HUGONIS (R. xanthina bugonis). Father Hugo's rose, golden rose of China

Yellow. Central China. In mid- to late spring, every branch is a garland of 2-inch, bright yellow, single blossoms with a light scent. After the petals drop, you're left with a shrub of great delicacy and beauty: an upright to arching plant to about 8 feet high, its branches clothed in locustlike leaves to 4 inches long, each with 5 to 11 nearly round leaflets less than an inch across. Pea-size, brownish red to maroon hips ripen in autumn.

ROSA LAEVIGATA. Cherokee rose

White. Southern China, Southeast Asia. This handsome species is widely naturalized throughout the southeastern United States; it has been made the state flower of Georgia, and a native Indian tribe features in its common name. For climates that never see winter temperatures lower than 0°F/−18°C, this rampant climber provides foliage in quantity—distinctive three-leafleted leaves with a glossy, lacquered look—and broad-petaled, elegant, 3½-inch white blossoms. The green stems are armed with tenacious hooked thorns.

ROSA MOSCHATA. Musk rose

White. Area of origin uncertain; risky in regions where winter temperatures regularly dip below 0°F/−18°C. This vigorous, arching shrub comes into flower later in spring than

TOP LEFT: *Rosa eglanteria*   TOP RIGHT: *Rosa foetida* 'Bicolor'
MIDDLE: *Rosa foetida* 'Bicolor' (and yellow reversions)
BOTTOM: *Rosa bugonis*

many other roses, but continues to bloom on and off through summer and into autumn until it is stopped by frost. Clustered ivory white, 2-inch single blossoms are intensely sweet scented; small, nearly round orange-red hips provide decoration in autumn and winter. The matte-finish, medium green foliage is especially dense; as a bonus, it turns butter yellow in late autumn. A double-flowered form, *R. m. plena,* is sometimes available.

ROSA MOYESII

Red or pink. Western China. Some would label this an awkward shrub, but its structure provides an excellent framework for displaying the distinctive flowers and hips. Large, loose, and rather sparse, it is best used as a background shrub or even a shrub-tree to 10 feet or so. An arresting profusion of brilliant red single flowers to 2½ inches across makes a show in spring; in autumn, bottle-shaped hips of blazing orange red dangle from the spreading branches. Two notable selections are 'Geranium' (with red flowers) and 'Sealing Wax' (with pink blooms), both of which are shorter and more compact than the species. *R. moyesii* and its varieties are roses for areas where winter low temperatures remain above −10°F/−23°C.

ROSA MULTIFLORA. Multiflora, Japanese rose

White. Japan, Korea. Like *R. canina,* this species has a history of gainful employment. In North America, it's a popular understock for commercial rose production; in parts of the Midwest and East, it was once recommended as a field-hedge plant, a wildlife cover, and even a freeway-median crash barrier! Long, arching canes form thicketlike mounds to 10 feet high and 15 feet across; softly downy foliage and large clusters of white, blackberrylike single flowers complete the picture. Its vigor is both an asset and a drawback: branches can root where they touch soil, making one plant a vast colony in time, and birds' fondness for the tiny hips means a profusion of volunteer seedlings in summer-rainfall (or summer-watered) climates. Thornless forms are sometimes available.

ROSA ROXBURGHII. Chestnut rose, chinquapin rose

Pink. Western China. The bristly, burrlike calyx from which the bud emerges gives this rose its common names. Established plants are stiff stemmed and large, to 10 feet or taller and 15 feet across; the older stems are covered in peeling cinnamon-colored bark. The light green leaves are composed of leaflets so small that the foliage has a ferny look. Two forms are available, both with lilac pink flowers. *R. roxburghii* is double flowered and looks rather like a tree peony; its blooms are packed with countless petals. The single-flowered form is *R. roxburghii normalis.*

TOP LEFT: *Rosa moyesii* (hips)   TOP RIGHT: *Rosa moyesii*
MIDDLE: *Rosa multiflora*
BOTTOM LEFT: *Rosa rugosa*   BOTTOM RIGHT: *Rosa roxburghii*

Rosa sericea pteracantha and *Geranium × oxonianum* 'Claridge Druce'

ROSA RUGOSA. Japanese rose, ramanas rose, sea tomato

White, purple, pink. Northeastern Asia, Japan. A hybridizer could hardly have designed a rose with more virtues. Vigorous plants reach just 3 to 8 feet high, spreading into colonies if grown on their own roots. The bright green, glossy leaves have a distinctive heavy veining that gives them a crinkled appearance—and best of all, they are nearly diseaseproof. Silky-petaled, 3- to 4-inch-wide flowers in several colors appear in spring, summer, and autumn. *R. r. alba* has single white blossoms; *R. r. rubra* has magenta purple single blooms, while *R. r. kamtchatica* bears lilac pink single flowers on a smaller plant overall. Specialty growers may offer double-flowered variants. Large, conspicuous orange hips develop throughout the flowering period on all forms. All rugosas are extremely tough and cold hardy, enduring hard freezes, aridity, wind, and salt spray. All are excellent hedge plants.

ROSA SERICEA PTERACANTHA

White. Southern China. Two features make this rose instantly recognizable. First, the single white flowers have just four petals rather than the customary five; and second, when you look past the flowers to the stems, you see the impressive broad-based thorns that march up the canes with scarcely a space between them. On first-year wood, the red-brown thorns are translucent. Leaves consist of up to 19 small leaflets that resemble boxwood foliage; their size and texture stand in almost startling contrast to the armature. The bushes are vigorous and arching, reaching a height of around 10 feet.

ROSA SPINOSISSIMA *(R. pimpinellifolia)*. Scotch rose, burnet rose

White or pink. Western Europe across Asia into China and Korea. This suckering, spreading rose produces upright, bristly-spiny canes to 4 feet, closely set with small, almost fernlike leaves (hence the common-name allusion to burnet). The 2-inch, single blossoms may be white or pink; they're followed by pealike, dark brown to black hips. 'Altaica' ('Grandiflora') has 3-inch, cream-colored flowers on a larger-leafed plant to 6 feet tall.

ROSA VIRGINIANA

Pink. Eastern North America. This elegant wildflower makes dense clumps of upright canes to about 6 feet high, well covered in handsome, nearly glossy leaves with elongated, 2-inch leaflets. After the clear pink, 2-inch single flowers fade, the plant bears a crop of small, round hips that turn red when ripe. Like many of the native trees and shrubs found growing with it in the wild, it mounts a bright autumn foliage display, in colors ranging from yellow through tawny gold to red.

Rosa spinosissima

GALLICA ROSES

In the wild, Rosa gallica is found in central, western, and southern Europe and in western Asia—the very territories where early western civilizations emerged. It can claim, therefore, to be perhaps the earliest rose to have been noticed, revered, and cultivated. Pliny's red "rose of Miletus" may well have been a form of R. gallica. Certainly by the Middle Ages various gallicas, particularly 'Apothecary's Rose', were grown for medicine and perfume. Commercial cultivation southeast of Paris led to an early name for the group: "rose of Provins."

Gallicas display the color red in all its manifestations: purple, magenta, crimson, cerise. The group also includes a few pink representatives and various elaborately to subtly striped and mottled combinations. The blossoms are notably fragrant; the plants are tough, vigorous, adaptable, and cold hardy.

Grown on their own roots, gallicas can spread into sizable colonies of stems; budded plants may grow larger than own-root bushes, but they won't sucker in the same fashion. Most are compact, upright, and only sparsely thorned, with outward- or upward-pointing foliage and flowers that also face upward.

ALAIN BLANCHARD (1839)

Red. Surrounding a prominent cluster of golden stamens are a few rows of petals—crimson when they unfold, mottled with maroon purple as they age, and quite purple by the time they fall. Stems are thornier than those of the average gallica, forming a mounding plant to about 4 to 5 feet high and wide.

APOTHECARY'S ROSE (ancient)

Red. Botanically, this is *Rosa gallica* 'Officinalis', the form cultivated by medieval herbalists—hence the popular name 'Apothecary's Rose'. The cherry crimson, semidouble blooms adorn an upright, bushy, 3- to 4-foot plant with dark foliage and few thorns. Grown on its own roots, it forms thick colonies of stems from the ground; with an annual trimming for uniform height, a row of plants makes a fine summer-flowering hedge.

TOP LEFT: Apothecary's Rose   TOP RIGHT: Belle de Crécy
MIDDLE: Cardinal de Richelieu
BOTTOM LEFT: Rosa Mundi   BOTTOM RIGHT: Superb Tuscan

BELLE DE CRÉCY (1829)

Pink to violet. The cherry pink buds hardly hint at the colors to follow: an intriguing Victorian medley of pink, lavender, soft violet, and gray, with the purple tones increasing as the blossoms open and age. Fully expanded flowers are packed with petals that often swirl around a central button eye. The nearly thornless stems may reach 4 feet, but the plants are not as sturdily upright as many other gallicas.

BELLE ISIS (1845)

Pink. Countless shell-like, soft pink petals fold and swirl into a flat flower of modest size and great charm. The pale color and thorny stems suggest something more than gallica ancestry, but the upright, 4-foot plant assorts perfectly with the other roses in this group.

CAMAIEUX (1830)

White, red, and purple. The informally double blossoms offer a striking patchwork quilt of harmonious colors. White to pale pink petals show crimson and pink stripes that change to lavender and grayed purple as the flowers age. Upright to arching stems may reach 4 feet, bearing grayed green leaves that complement the blossoms.

CARDINAL DE RICHELIEU (1840)

Purple. Rounded buds in small clusters open to rosy violet flowers that become almost ball-shaped at maturity—at which time the shell-like petals are smoky purple with silvery reverses. Nearly thornless, arching stems clothed in smooth green leaves form a rounded, dense bush to about 4 feet high.

CHARLES DE MILLS (circa 1840)

Red violet. A heady fragrance rises from flat, full-petaled crimson flowers that reveal tints of purple, lavender, and pink. When fully open, the blossoms are circular, often showing a button eye in the center of the folded, swirling petals. Dark foliage adorns a 5-foot, nearly thornless plant.

CONDITORUM
(ancient)

Red. The not-quite-double flowers resemble those of 'Tuscany' in form. In color, they fall between 'Tuscany' and 'Apothecary's Rose': rich crimson with the occasional purple tint, the golden stamens showing in the open blossom. Upright, bushy plants grow to about 3 feet high. Sometimes called "Hungarian rose," this is the variety grown in Hungary for the production of rose attar.

Charles de Mills

DUCHESSE DE MONTEBELLO (1829)

Pink. Arching, spreading growth and pale, clear blush pink blossoms point to more than gallica in the family tree, but this rose's general character and style place it among these more colorful compatriots. The fairly small flowers, packed full of neatly arranged petals, are carried in small clusters against a backdrop of foliage in a light gray green.

GLOIRE DE FRANCE (1819)

Pink. As exceptional as the name implies! The lilac pink blooms are packed with petals folded and gathered around a central eye; as they open, the center remains darker while the outer petals pale to nearly white. Dark green leaves cover a 3-foot shrub that spreads wider than it is high.

LA BELLE SULTANE (before 1700)

Red. With a plant that can reach up to 6 feet, this one stands out from its gallica cohorts. The rich crimson flowers are nearly single; as they age, purple tones overwhelm the red—accounting for another name, 'Violacea'. The nearly thornless stems are lightly clothed in drooping leaves.

NESTOR (1840s)

Magenta blend. Call the background color pink or light red—but in either case, it is so heavily infused with purple that the elaborately folded and quartered blooms may look predominantly lilac, lavender, or mauve. All this changeable beauty comes on a virtually thornless plant to about 4 feet tall.

ROSA MUNDI (ancient)

Red, pink, and white. It resembles 'Apothecary's Rose' done up as a peppermint stick—and indeed, 'Rosa Mundi' (botanically known as *Rosa gallica* 'Versicolor') is a sport of 'Apothecary's Rose', identical to it all respects save the flowers, which are irregularly striped, dashed, and flecked pink and red on a background of white. Not infrequently, a solid cherry red blossom appears that attests to the plant's origin. Legend has it that the rose was named after Fair Rosamond, the mistress of Henry II (king of England from 1154 to 1189).

SUPERB TUSCAN (before 1837)

Dark red. Many catalogs list this as 'Tuscany Superb'. Wavy petals that look to be cut from maroon velvet form a semi-double, perfumed blossom centered with a cluster of gold stamens. Plants are upright (to around 4 feet), thickly clothed with rich green leaves on stems with few thorns. Compared to 'Tuscany', this variety has larger leaves and larger blossoms with more petals.

TUSCANY (before 1596)

Dark red. The semidouble, velvety maroon red blooms resemble those of 'Superb Tuscan', though they are a bit smaller. The most notable difference between the two varieties, however, is that 'Tuscany' has fewer petals—making the golden stamens a more prominent feature. The upright, 4-foot plants spread to form sizable colonies.

DAMASK ROSES

Among the old garden groups, the damasks rank with the gallicas as the oldest roses known—and indeed, modern research places Rosa gallica *in their ancestry. Their most notable attribute is intense fragrance, a trait that brought them to the attention of the first Mediterranean and Near Eastern cultures and led to their early domestication as a cultivated crop. Even today, acres of summer damasks are grown in Bulgaria, Turkey, Iran, India, northern Africa, and southern France for use in the production of attar of roses.*

Two distinct damask types existed in ancient times and persist to this day. The larger group is the summer damasks (probably deriving in part from R. phoenicia), *varieties with a single annual late-spring flowering. The autumn damask group contains just one rose, closely related to the summer damasks but noteworthy for its repeat bloom: it flowers not only in spring, but also off and on through summer and autumn. This individual is thought to have* R. moschata, *the musk rose, in its parentage.*

All damasks typically have grayish, softly downy, rather elongated and pointed leaves; the canes tend to be thorny, often bearing both large thorns and smaller prickles. Summer damask roses form attractive bushes that arch and mound to around 5 feet high. 'Autumn Damask' has sparser foliage and a more upright habit; it's a somewhat lanky bush, best used among better-foliaged companions.

AUTUMN DAMASK (ancient)
Pink. Its botanical name is *Rosa × damascena* 'Bifera' ('Semperflorens'), but it goes by several more euphonious common names, including "quatre saisons" ("four seasons"), "rose of Paestum," and "rose of Castile." Slender buds with notably long sepals open to loose, highly scented blossoms in clear pink. After the spring flowering, it continues to bloom sporadically until stopped by cold weather. The plant is large, open, and thorny, with light gray-green foliage.

CELSIANA (before 1750)
Pink. Adorning a somewhat lax bush to about 5 feet tall are small clusters of large blossoms: intensely fragrant, semidouble, and soft pink, composed of silky, ruffled petals surrounding a central cluster of yellow stamens.

GLOIRE DE GUILAN (date unknown)
Pink. This is an old damask variety, grown in northern Iran for the production of attar of roses; in 1949, it was taken from there to England and christened with the above name. The clear soft pink blossoms are extremely double and quartered—and, of course, highly fragrant. The spreading, 4-foot-tall plant is clothed in apple green foliage.

TOP: Autumn Damask
MIDDLE: Celsiana
BOTTOM: Marie Louise

Ispahan

HEBE'S LIP (before 1846)

White and red. This rose is also known as 'Rubrotincta', a name that aptly describes its distinctive coloration: the creamy white petals are tipped and margined in rosy red. The flower is barely more than single and shows a central cluster of stamens. It is probably a damask hybrid, possibly with *R. eglanteria* (see page 16), and forms a stocky, upright plant with tooth-edged, fresh green leaves.

ISPAHAN (before 1832)

Pink. Clusters of double, clear medium pink blooms appear over a notably long season, opening flat from especially lovely buds. The plant is upright to around 6 feet high; the slightly glossy foliage and reduced number of thorns suggest an ancestry that is not entirely damask.

KAZANLIK (old; date unknown)

Pink. Also known as *Rosa damascena trigintipetala*, this sumptuously fragrant damask is grown extensively in Bulgaria for the production of attar of roses. Borne in small clusters, the warm medium pink blooms are loosely double, with stamens showing in the center. The upright plant can reach 7 feet high if given a bit of support.

LA VILLE DE BRUXELLES (1849)

Pink. A prickly-stemmed bush with elegantly elongated leaves bears large, rich pink blooms of superb form. Each flower opens flat, the outermost petals seeming to form a shallow saucer holding countless elaborately folded petals arranged around a button eye. The plant is upright to about 5 feet, becoming rather spreading when freighted with blossoms.

LEDA (before 1827)

White. Crimson markings on the tips of the blush to white petals have given this rose the common name "painted damask." Countless petals, often surrounding a button eye, compose a symmetrical blossom that can become nearly ball-like when fully expanded. 'Pink Leda' (before 1844)

is a pink-flowered form. The bush is a compact grower to about 4 feet, clothed in dark green foliage.

MARIE LOUISE (1813)

Deep pink. Grown at Malmaison in the time of Empress Josephine, this exquisite damask is still treasured today for its very large, very full, fragrant blossoms of deep carmine pink. Each flower unfolds to become circular and flat, centered with a button eye of smaller petals. Naturally arching and spreading in form, the plant may reach 4 feet high— but during bloom time, it's usually weighed down by its blossoms.

MME. HARDY (1832)

White. Its special beauty is in its open flowers: cupped to flat, each packed with symmetrically arranged, pristine white petals around a green center. Clusters of these fragrant blossoms decorate a moderately tall plant (to 6 feet) with leaves that are darker and broader than is typical of most damasks.

MME. ZÖETMANS (1830)

White. This one rivals 'Mme. Hardy' in floral perfection, but its flowers may be the palest blush pink—fading to creamy white and exposing a green central eye as they age. Foliage of fresh, clear green covers a spreading bush that may reach 4 feet high.

YORK AND LANCASTER (before 1629)

White and pink. Though properly called *Rosa × damascena* 'Versicolor', this rose is almost universally known by the name commemorating the two opposing royal houses in the Wars of the Roses. The loosely double blossoms may be pinkish white, light to medium pink, or a pink-and-white combination; all three variations sometimes appear in a single flower cluster. The plant is fairly tall (to 6 or 7 feet), with grayish leaves and plentiful thorns.

Mme. Hardy

ALBA ROSES

The original alba roses were natural hybrids, thought to be derived from the damask rose and a white form of the dog rose (Rosa canina). The combination sweetened the damask parent's tangy perfume and produced long-lived, sparsely thorned plants of vigorous, upright habit and exceptional disease resistance. Of the early forms of Rosa × alba, *just a few remain in cultivation—but these include some of the most valuable old roses for garden decoration. All the albas flower only once annually, in spring. The single to very double blossoms, in white or delicate tints of pink, are beautifully displayed against a backdrop of plentiful gray-green foliage. Most of these roses tolerate some shade; the bushes can serve as self-supporting shrubs, as pseudo-climbers attached to fences or walls, or even as bedding roses if pruned fairly heavily.*

ALBA MAXIMA (ancient)

White. One of the oldest albas, this rose has gone by a number of other names over the years, among them "Cheshire rose," "great double white," "Jacobite rose," and simply *Rosa alba maxima*. It's a tall bush (to 8 feet) with dull, dark gray-green leaves that are borne more heavily in the plant's upper reaches. The loosely double flowers, carried in small clusters, come in pure to creamy white.

ALBA SEMI-PLENA (before 1867)

White. As the name suggests, the flowers are less than double—but they are no less beautiful for that fact. The blossoms, each consisting of several rows of pure white petals surrounding a central clump of golden stamens, are scattered like a light snowfall over an arching, 6-foot shrub with the typical gray-green alba foliage. Red hips decorate the branches in autumn.

BELLE AMOUR (old; date unknown)

Pink. An air of mystery surrounds this alba: it was found growing in a French convent, but its true origin is unknown. It differs from other albas in its warm pink color and spicy fragrance, but the 7-foot shrub with good foliage is typical of the group. When fully open, the blossoms reveal a central brush of golden stamens.

Celestial

CELESTIAL (before 1848)

Pink. The soft, milky pink blooms range from double to somewhat less than double, and often show a central cluster of golden stamens. The plant is tall and upright growing (to 7 feet), with red-tinted rather than green stems and the typical gray-toned alba foliage.

CHLORIS (before 1848)

Pink. Dark green leaves—the darkest found on any alba—set this rose apart. Flesh pink, satiny petals swirl around a button eye in each small flower. The nearly thornless bushes are upright and fairly compact, and may reach a height of 5 feet.

FÉLICITÉ PARMENTIER (before 1834)

Pale pink. Packed with petals, the flowers are cupped when they first unfold, then open to a rounded shape; the color fades from soft pink to nearly white. Distinctly grayed foliage clothes a medium-size plant reaching 4 to 5 feet tall.

GREAT MAIDEN'S BLUSH (well before 1738)

Pink-tinted white. This lovely antique has been known by various names, including *Rosa alba incarnata* and the more suggestive 'La Séduisante' and 'Cuisse de Nymphe.' Plentiful gray-green foliage clothes a large (to 7-foot-tall) shrub that arches under the weight of its clustered full, milky blush pink blossoms.

JEANNE D'ARC (1818)

White. More spreading and twiggy than the general run of albas, this rose reaches a height of perhaps 5 feet and bears creamy white blossoms packed with petals; overall, it looks something like a smaller version of 'Alba Maxima'. Foliage is darker than that of the average alba and not quite as disease resistant.

KÖNIGIN von DÄNEMARK (1826)

Pink. As each bud opens, the multitudinous deep pink petals form a cup-shaped flower which expands and reflexes to become nearly flat, exposing a central button eye. The petal margins fade to pale pink with age. An arching bush to about 5 feet tall, it's a bit thornier than other albas, with coarser, blue-gray foliage.

MAIDEN'S BLUSH (1797)

Pink-tinted white. Sometimes called 'Small Maiden's Blush' to distinguish it from 'Great Maiden's Blush'. In comparison to the latter, this is a smaller bush (reaching only about 4 feet), with slightly smaller blossoms of the same milky pale pink.

TOP LEFT: Alba Maxima   TOP RIGHT: Alba Semi-Plena
BOTTOM LEFT: Königin von Dänemark   BOTTOM RIGHT: Félicité Parmentier

MME. LEGRAS DE ST. GERMAIN (1846)

White. Each elegant flower is a symmetrical construction of countless ivory white petals shading to pale yellow in the center. Borne in clusters, the blossoms are complemented by the typical grayed alba foliage. Grown as a shrub, the plant can reach 7 feet; if encouraged to grow as a climber, it can attain about twice that height.

POMPON BLANC PARFAIT (1876)

Pale pink. A comparatively recent member of the group, this charming alba departs from the typical mold. Its small, very double blossoms, in pale pink fading to white, are produced in tight clusters over a long flowering period. The gray-green leaves are correspondingly small, adorning a compact, upright shrub to about 4 feet tall.

CENTIFOLIA ROSES

Cabbage Rose   Cristata

Derivatives of the albas and damasks, the centifolias are known for their lush blossoms: centifolia *literally means "hundred-leafed," a reference to the countless petals—certainly 100 or more—contained in each bloom. The variety 'Cabbage Rose' is one of the best-known members of the group. Indeed, "cabbage rose" has become a common name for the class as a whole, a general description of the archetypal round blossoms: great globes consisting of large outer petals which, as the flower opens, cradle the multitude of smaller petals within.*

The springtime blossoms are intensely fragrant, still the main source of true rose essence for the French perfume industry. Colors include all shades of pink; a few varieties offer white or red-violet blooms. The leaves are characteristically drooping, each consisting of broad, rounded leaflets. The larger-growing varieties have lax, thorny canes that arch or sprawl with the weight of the heavy blossoms; you can drape them over a low fence as semiclimbers or give them a support (such as wire or wooden "cages") from which the flower-laden stems can spill.

BLANCHEFLEUR (1835)

White. Light green foliage makes a clean backdrop for creamy white, petal-packed blossoms that open from red-tipped buds. The blossoms are sometimes quartered and become flat when fully expanded. The vigorous, prickly canes reach 5 to 6 feet tall.

BULLATA (before 1815)

Pink. The colloquial name for this one is "lettuce-leafed rose," an apt description of the leaflets: each is very broad and puckered, looking almost as if it needed ironing. The bush is arching and about 5 feet high, its stems less thorny than those of most other centifolias. The medium pink, bowl-shaped blossoms are essentially identical to those of 'Cabbage Rose', from which 'Bullata' probably sported. (Turn to page 8 for a Pierre-Joseph Redouté portrait of this rose.)

CABBAGE ROSE (before 1600)

Pink. Here is the archetype of the class: *Rosa × centifolia,* also known by the name "Provence rose." Medium pink, bowl-shaped blossoms packed with countless petals appear on arching, thorny, 5- to 6-foot canes decked out in coarse gray-green foliage.

CRISTATA (1827)

Pink. The elaborately fringed calyx, so visible in unopened buds, accounts for the common name "crested moss" (under which this unique rose is frequently sold). Another name, "chapeau de Napoleon," comes from the buds' supposed resemblance to the French emperor's tricorne hat. Common names notwithstanding, 'Cristata' is not a true moss rose, since only the calyx edges are fringed, giving the bud the look of a floral chestnut burr. From this rococo cocoon emerges a typical full, cupped centifolia blossom in silvery pink. The bush is upright to 6 feet tall, with light green foliage.

FANTIN-LATOUR (date unknown)

Pink. Tradition places this rose among the centifolias, but its country and date of origin are a mystery, and its ancestry may involve more than centifolia: it has fewer thorns and larger, darker leaves than the usual. The sumptuous blossoms are large, full, and rich soft pink; they open cup shaped, then reflex to show a buttonlike center. Arching canes form a tall bush to around 6 feet high.

Fantin-Latour

JUNO (before 1832)

Pink. Like 'Fantin-Latour', this appears to have more than *Rosa × centifolia* in its makeup, but its flowers and growth habit are solidly centifolia. Fragrant, blush pink blossoms are packed with petals and show a button eye when fully

Paul Ricault   Tour de Malakoff

expanded. Grayish green leaves adorn a fairly lax and spreading plant to about 4 feet high.

LA NOBLESSE (1856)

Pink. This rose is a good season-extender, since it's probably the last centifolia to come into bloom. Typical centifolia blossoms—rich pink and fragrant, loaded with petals and opening out flat—are produced on a plant to about 5 feet tall, more compact in form than most members of the class.

PAUL RICAULT (1845)

Deep pink. Depth of color and depth of fragrance merge in a silken blossom with countless petals that may be arranged in quartered fashion. The 5- to 6-foot plant, covered in good dark green foliage, is upright growing but can be weighed down by its wealth of flowers during bloom time.

PETITE DE HOLLANDE (1800)

Pink. In all respects, this is a scaled-down version of 'Cabbage Rose'. Soft pink, ultra-double blossoms are a bit under 2 inches across but produce a full-size fragrance. Leaves are correspondingly small, while the 3- to 4-foot plant is more upright, stiff, and compact than the larger-growing members of the group.

POMPON DE BOURGOGNE (1664)

Dark pink. This little centifolia has gone by a number of names over the centuries; you may also find it catalogued as 'Burgundian Rose'. Clumps of upright, nearly thornless stems to about 3 feet bear inch-wide rosettes in carmine pink with purple shadings. The dark gray-green leaves are likewise small.

ROBERT LE DIABLE (before 1837)

Red violet. These arresting blossoms show gallica influence. As petal-packed as a typical centifolia, they open to a more spherical shape, with outer petals reflexing and central petals remaining more upright. The color, too brings a gallica to mind: a changeable, hard-to-capture mix of crimson, violet, gray, and lilac, varying with the weather and expo-

sure. Plants reach 3 to 4 feet high; if grown on their own roots, they form gallica-like colonies.

ROSE DE MEAUX (1789)

Pink. Truly a miniature centifolia, this diminutive charmer is an upright, bushy plant just 2 feet high and wide. Perfect little pompon-style flowers—only an inch across—are emphatically fragrant, their petals a clear, unshaded pink. The sport 'White Rose de Meaux' (before 1799) is identical but for its white blossoms with pink-tinted centers.

ROSE DES PEINTRES (before 1800)

Pink. Here is the typical pink centifolia, the rose often seen in 16th- and 17th-century Dutch and Flemish floral still-lifes. Usually described as an "improved" 'Cabbage Rose', it offers similar rich pink flowers on a slightly taller plant with darker foliage.

THE BISHOP (date unknown)

Red violet. Plant this atypical variety for a harmonious color variation among the prevailingly pink centifolias. A slender, upright bush to about 4 feet tall bears scented rosettes that open cerise to magenta, then age to shades of violet and gray.

TOUR DE MALAKOFF (1856)

Magenta. The tallest of the centifolias, this one produces canes to about 8 feet long, which, like the stems of climbing roses, benefit from support or training. The large blossoms are loosely double (sometimes showing a few stamens) and turn increasingly purple with age; old blossoms may be shades of grape and lilac.

UNIQUE BLANCHE (1775)

White. Silky-sheened petals form a flower that starts out cup shaped but finishes as a flat bloom with a central button eye. In fully open flowers, the petals are less formally arranged than is typical of most other centifolias. The plant, though, is a standard centifolia bush to about 5 feet high and wide.

Rose de Meaux

MOSS ROSES

Most of the noteworthy mutations in the world of roses involve petals—their color, size, or number. The moss roses, though, are distinguished by a change in the floral "envelope": the calyx enclosing the bud (and the pedicel supporting it) are covered in decorative mossy glands. The original moss rose appeared as a mutation on a centifolia, and many of the choicest varieties are simply centifolias with that mossy detail. But hybridizing of centifolia mosses with other classes has produced repeat-blooming moss roses that flower again after the initial spring flush. A few mossy sports have appeared on damask roses, too, but the difference is apparent to the touch: a centifolia moss is soft, while a damask one is distinctly prickly.

ALFRED DE DALMAS (1855)

Pink. Borne on a 4-foot bush, the creamy pink, moderately full flowers with shell-shaped petals have a porcelainlike delicacy and a pleasant perfume. Buds are lightly covered in light green to pink moss. Plants bloom sporadically after the spring show.

COMMUNIS (1696)

Pink. Also known as 'Common Moss' and *Rosa × centifolia muscosa*, this is the original centifolia mutation, with balsam-scented green moss covering the buds and pedicels. The flower is a typical highly scented, full-petaled, pink centifolia that starts out cupped, then opens flat with a button eye. The moderately tall, open-structured plant blooms in spring, at the same time as the other centifolias.

COMTESSE DE MURINAIS (1843)

Pale pink. Damask moss. The cupped to flat, full-petaled flowers go through a delicate change of color, paling from flesh pink to creamy white with age. The plentiful prickly green moss is highly scented; the leaves are light green. The plant is fairly tall—to around 6 feet—and does best with support.

DEUIL DE PAUL FONTAINE (1873)

Red. Damask moss. This repeat bloomer features round, mossy buds that open to 2-inch flowers packed with petals

Salet

of an unusual purplish red with brown shading. The plant is moderate in size.

GLOIRE DES MOUSSEUX (1852)

Pink. Buds heavily cloaked in green moss unfold to really large, deep pink blossoms that pale to lighter tones at the petal margins. The upright plant grows 4 to 5 feet high; the foliage is light green.

HENRI MARTIN (1863)

🌹 Red. Damask moss. Lightly mossed, semidouble blooms are a rich, clear crimson, turning deep rose pink with age. These fragrant beauties are borne in great profusion on a 5-foot, arching plant with wiry stems and fresh green leaves.

MME. LOUIS LÉVÊQUE (1898)

🌹 Pink. Large, cupped blossoms in silvery, satiny pink look like those of a hybrid perpetual (see pages 38–39) with a light encrustation of moss for decoration. The flowers are highly fragrant, appearing on a moderately tall (about 6-foot), upright plant that blooms again after the spring show.

NUITS DE YOUNG (1845)

🌹 Maroon. A striking flower: velvety, purple-shaded petals with nearly black recesses are accented by a few golden stamens. Decked out in dark-tinted moss, the fairly small blooms are borne on a wiry, upright-growing, 4-foot plant with small, dark green leaves.

SALET (1854)

🌹 Pink. This one offers steadier, less sporadic repeat flowering than most of the other repeat-blooming mosses. Its informal, full, deep pink blossoms show a moderate amount of moss. The plant has soft green leaves and few thorns; it reaches about 4 feet high.

WHITE BATH (1810)

🌹 White. This lovely specimen has been known by numerous names, among them "Climton rose," "Shailer's white moss," and *Rosa × centifolia muscosa alba*. A sport of the original moss rose 'Communis', it is nearly identical to it save for its white flowers.

WILLIAM LOBB (1855)

🌹 Dark red. This rose is also known as "old velvet moss," a name that well describes the rich mix of magenta, crimson, purple, and lilac in the heavily mossed, semidouble blossoms. The tall, rangy plant reaches around 8 feet and does best if given support or treated as a climber.

Gloire des Mousseaux

TOP: Mme. Louis Lévêque
MIDDLE: White Bath
BOTTOM: Alfred de Dalmas

CHINA ROSES

The first China roses to arrive in Europe were the product of centuries of work by Chinese horticulturists, who selected and preserved superior forms of Rosa chinensis *for their own gardens. To Europeans, the novelty of these roses lay in their ability to flower repeatedly, in flush after flush, from spring until stopped by autumn frosts; in the warm-winter gardens of the French and Italian Riviera, they bloomed virtually all year round.*

Chinas are the main source of repeat flowering in modern roses. In the plants, you first see what resembles a modern rose bush: upright to vase shaped or rounded, with smooth, elongated leaflets and fairly stiff stems that terminate in one blossom or a cluster of several blooms. The flowers are fairly small, just 2 to 3 inches in diameter, and their color darkens rather than fades with exposure to sunlight (a trait unique to the China roses).

These are plants for the South, Southwest, and West, wherever winter temperatures reliably remain above 5°F/–15°C. (In colder areas, Chinas need the same sort of winter protection hybrid teas require.) Remarkably, the two original imports from China are still available for planting today.

ARCHDUKE CHARLES (before 1837)

Pink to red. These full flowers clearly display the China rose characteristic of darkening with exposure to sun. On overcast days or in light shade, the prevailing color is pink. When sunlight strikes the petals, though, the pink quickly turns to rosy red—yet where petals overlap, the covered part remains pink. The plants are bushy and somewhat rounded, to about 3 feet high.

COMTESSE DU CAYLA (1902)

Orange blend. Semidouble blossoms open coral orange centered with yellow, then age to salmon pink. When young, the plants are twiggy, with a mounded to spreading form; once established, they can become 6-foot mounds of bronze to green leaves. Flowers have better quality and color where summers are not hot and dry.

TOP LEFT: Hermosa   TOP RIGHT: Setina (climbing form of 'Hermosa')
MIDDLE: Louis Philippe
BOTTOM LEFT: Cramoisi Supérieur   BOTTOM RIGHT: Old Blush

CRAMOISI SUPÉRIEUR (1832)

Red. Also known as 'Agrippina'. Plump, small buds open to full, symmetrical blossoms of glowing ruby red, which hold their color until the petals drop. The bush is fairly low, mounded, and twiggy, but it can reach 4 feet or more with age. There is a vigorous climbing form.

DUCHER (1869)

White. Lovely buds about 1½ inches long open to nearly double, somewhat cupped blossoms in pure white. Clothed in leaves that age from bronzy-hued to green, the bush is upright growing (to about 4 feet) and less angular in form than many other Chinas.

HERMOSA (before 1837)

Pink. Pure, unshaded, cake-frosting pink blossoms are symmetrical, somewhat cupped, and about 2½ inches wide, borne in clusters that recall some of the damasks or mosses. Smallish, gray-green leaves cover a vigorous, bushy, thorny plant that, in time, can build to a dense 4 to 6 feet. There is a vigorous climbing form, 'Setina' (1879); it flowers mainly in spring.

LOUIS PHILIPPE (1834)

Red. This one offers all you might want in vigor and profuse bloom. The bush is large, open, and broadly vase-shaped, reminiscent of a tumbleweed in its shape and density. Rather small, pink-centered red blossoms with shell-shaped petals come in clusters. In the South, this variety has been used for hedge planting.

MME. LAURETTE MESSIMY (1887)

Salmon. Loosely semidouble flowers open from shapely buds; they start out salmon, then turn to warm pink. Though it bears some resemblance to 'Comtesse du Cayla', this rose is a smaller plant with paler blossoms.

MUTABILIS (before 1894)

Buff, pink, and red. This is a true individual, different from other Chinas and, in plant, showing considerable tea rose influence. From buff yellow buds, the five-petaled single blossoms open buff, then turn pink, and finally age to a light wine red. Plants showing all three colors at once seem to be covered with a swarm of butterflies. The bush is wide spreading, rounded, and definitely large, with main canes that become thick and woody in time; it can even be trained against a wall in the manner of a climber.

OLD BLUSH (ancient; introduced to England by 1792)

Pink. Christened 'Parson's Pink China' when it arrived in England from the Orient, this is the first China rose to be brought to Europe. Shapely, 1½-inch buds open to informal rose pink blossoms that become shaded and mottled with darker pink to rosy red as they age. The plant is upright to about 3 feet high. There is a rampant climbing form that blooms only sparsely after the spring flush.

SLATER'S CRIMSON CHINA (ancient; introduced to England by 1792)

Red. The second of the original imports from China, this one has informal semidouble blossoms of clear, unshaded red. Always spangled with these cheery blooms, the 3-foot plant is slender stemmed and not especially dense.

Mutabilis

PORTLAND ROSES

The revolution that ultimately led to the plethora of modern varieties began with these roses—the first group to be developed through breeding with the repeat-flowering Asian types. Popularly called Portland roses in homage to 'Duchess of Portland', the first of the group, they also were known as "perpetual damasks"—a name that hints at their character. Though ancestries appear to vary a bit, all Portlands seem to have been derived in part from 'Autumn Damask' and the China roses, in particular 'Slater's Crimson China'. The resulting hybrids combine the full-petaled floral style (and fragrance) of once-blooming European classes with the repeat bloom of the Chinas. The plants are fairly short and shrubby, even stiff; many show the damask characteristic of bearing foliage right up to the base of the flower to form a leafy collar.

COMTE DE CHAMBORD (1860)

Pink. Plentiful repeat flowering reveals China heritage, but in all other respects, this rose might as well be a damask or gallica. Upright 3-foot plants with light green leaves produce petal-crammed blooms in a luscious rich pink; the flowers start out cupped, then open flat, even quartered, to reveal a button eye.

DUCHESS OF PORTLAND (about 1800)

Red. The founding mother of the group bears semidouble, bright cherry crimson blossoms on a broadly upright, 3-foot plant with medium green foliage.

MARBRÉE (1858)

Crimson. The color frustrates description—maybe purplish pink, maybe blue-toned red, with attractive blush pink marbling on the petals. The blossoms are only lightly scented; though more double than those of 'Duchess of Portland', they are still informally arranged. Upright, dark-foliaged plants reach about 4 feet.

MARCHESA BOCCELLA (1842)

Pink. Also known as 'Marquise Boçella' and 'Jacques Cartier'. It's similar in color and style to 'Comte de Chambord', but the flowers reflex a bit toward a pompon shape

TOP: Comte de Chambord
BOTTOM LEFT: Marchesa Boccella   BOTTOM RIGHT: Rose du Roi

and have a generally shaggier appearance. Dark, leathery foliage clothes an upright, 3-foot bush.

ROSE DE RESCHT (date unknown)

Crimson purple. These little pompons pack a powerful fragrance. Borne in clusters, they bloom continuously on a bushy, upright, 3-foot plant densely clothed in grayed green leaves.

ROSE DU ROI (1815)

Red. Fat buds open to fragrant, loosely double flowers of bright crimson with purple shadings. The bushy plant reaches about 3 feet high and wide. A lovely garden ornament, this rose has great historic importance: it passed along its color and scent to its red hybrid perpetual descendants (see pages 38–39), which in turn were the forebears of the red hybrid teas.

ROSE DU ROI À FLEUR POURPRES (1819)

Red violet. Considered a sport of 'Rose du Roi' and virtually identical to it, save for flowers that are a bit more double and definitely a darker red, with a strong infusion of purple.

BOURBON ROSES

In the hands of European breeders, a hybrid found growing in the hedgerows of the Île de Bourbon (now Réunion) begat a group known simply as Bourbons. Though their individual ancestries include other roses and rose classes, these Bourbons form a distinct group that foreshadowed the hybrid perpetuals (see pages 38–39). From the China side of the Bourbon equation came silken petals and reliable repeat flowering; from the 'Autumn Damask' parent came intense fragrance and larger plants, many of which might be called semi-climbers.

HONORINE DE BRABANT (date unknown)

Pale pink. The light pink to nearly white petals are irregularly striped in purplish pink to violet, but the effect is harmonious rather than garish. Full, cupped blossoms are borne on a fairly tall plant (to about 6 feet) with thick foliage and few thorns.

LOUISE ODIER (1851)

Pink. Full-petaled, cupped to camellialike blossoms in bright, deep pink have a pronounced fragrance. A vigorous plant to about 5 feet tall, this rose may be used as an upright (pillar-type) climber, but the canes must be securely tied if they're not to be weighed down by their heavy flower clusters.

MME. ISAAC PEREIRE (1881)

Violet pink. Everything about this rose says "big"—including its intoxicating fragrance. Full-petaled blossoms of an intense purplish pink are backed by large leaves on a plant so vigorous it is better used as a small climber. In its sport 'Mme. Ernst Calvat' (1888), the flower color is softened to a silvery light raspberry pink.

REINE VICTORIA (1872)

Pink. Also sold as 'La Reine Victoria'. Shell-like, silky, rich pink petals form cupped, globular, fragrant, medium-size flowers, carried in small clusters on a slender, 6-foot bush with elegant-looking soft green leaves. 'Mme. Pierre Oger' (1878) is a sport of 'Reine Victoria', differing only in flower color: its blossoms are ivory to palest pink, their petals edged in darker pink.

SOUVENIR DE LA MALMAISON (1843)

Light pink. The flat, circular, soft pink flowers are so full of petals they might pass for centifolias—in fact, they are so double that they may not open fully in damp climates. The rounded, hybrid tea–like bush often establishes slowly, but eventually reaches 4 feet; the climbing sport (see page 77) is especially vigorous. There is a creamy white sport, 'Kronprinzessin Viktoria' (1887), as well as a dark pink to rosy red sport (1845) sold as 'Red Souvenir de la Malmaison', 'Souvenir de la Malmaison Rouge', or 'Lewison Gower'.

VARIEGATA DI BOLOGNA (1909)

White and red. Cupped, double blossoms to 4 inches across flaunt a peppermint-stick combination of white petals striped purplish red. Borne in small clusters, the flowers appear primarily in spring; repeat bloom is spotty. The plant is tall and vigorous; it can be trained as a pillar-climber or simply allowed to become a 6-foot fountain of canes.

ZÉPHIRINE DROUHIN (1868)

Pink. Though tradition places it in the class, this rose is probably not "pure" Bourbon—its thornless canes and autumn foliage color suggest the influence of the Boursault rose, *R. × l'heritierana*. Semidouble to loosely double, cerise pink flowers adorn the plant like a flight of butterflies. It's naturally a restrained climber (to 8 to 12 feet)—but if a climber would be too large for your available space, treat it as a large shrub. 'Martha' (1912) and 'Kathleen Harrop' (1919) are light pink sports.

TOP LEFT: Honorine de Brabant   TOP RIGHT: Mme. Isaac Pereire
BOTTOM LEFT: Reine Victoria   BOTTOM RIGHT: Mme. Pierre Oger (sport of 'Reine Victoria')

NOISETTE ROSES

Whether it arose through deliberate hybridization or as a chance seedling, the first Noisette rose appeared at the plantation of South Carolina rice grower John Champneys. Known as 'Champneys' Pink Cluster', it was a cross of the musk rose (Rosa moschata) and the China variety 'Old Blush'. Champneys' neighbor, Philippe Noisette, sent seeds (or seedlings) from the Champneys plant to his brother in Paris; the rose raised from these was the first to bear the Noisette name, which was then applied to the race soon derived from it. The original Noisettes were shrubby semi-climbers that were virtually everblooming, bearing small, clustered flowers. Crossed to various tea roses (see page 36), they gave rise to the larger-flowered tea-Noisettes—definite climbers with blooms mainly in luscious shades of yellow, salmon, and buff orange. Abundant bloom and good, plentiful foliage is typical of both Noisettes and tea-Noisettes. These are choice plants for fairly mild-winter regions (temperatures no lower than about 10°F/−12°C), where they stand little danger of being killed by frosts.

Lamarque

AIMÉE VIBERT (1828)

White. Small, pure white, very double blossoms (sometimes with a button eye) come in large clusters on a plant clothed in light green leaves with notably elongated leaflets. The original plant was a low-growing shrub, recently rediscovered and reintroduced into the nursery trade. More frequently sold is 'Aimée Vibert Scandens' (1841), a large, angular climber. Flowering starts in late spring and continues for the rest of the growing season.

ALISTER STELLA GRAY (1894)

Yellow. Clusters of shapely yellow buds open to full, medium-size, orange-centered flowers that fade to cream. The very vigorous plant produces long-lived, long primary canes which give rise to shrubbier secondary growth.

BLUSH NOISETTE (1817)

Pink. The first rose to carry the Noisette name. Sizable clusters of small, rounded buds open to full, fragrant pink blossoms. The plant is mounding and semiclimbing.

CHAMPNEYS' PINK CLUSTER (1811)

Pink. The progenitor of all Noisette roses. Like its offspring 'Blush Noisette', it's a shrubby semiclimber bearing clusters of small flowers. The notably sweet-scented blooms are semidouble, with overlapping petals; the color is palest pink.

CRÉPUSCULE (1904)

Orange blend. The name means "twilight" in French—but this is the sun's final blaze, not the end-of-day purple shadows. Clusters of small orange buds open to medium-size blooms of bright saffron salmon, fading to buff. The plant is a shrubby climber, well clothed in small leaves.

JAUNE DESPREZ (1830)

Yellow and pink. Perhaps the first offspring derived from crossing 'Blush Noisette' with a yellow tea rose, this long-caned, limber plant bears clusters of double, medium-small flowers in salmon, nearly orange, yellow, or a combination of colors, depending on the weather.

LAMARQUE (1830)

White. Plenty of pointed, medium green leaves clothe this vigorous, far-reaching yet dense climber. Bloom time brings a lavish display of powerfully sweet-scented blossoms: small clusters of fully double, medium-size flowers in creamy white to palest lemon, opening from shapely buds.

MARÉCHAL NIEL (1864)

Yellow. Probably the most famous Noisette, beloved since its introduction for its large, beautifully shaped, highly fragrant blossoms of soft medium yellow that face downward from pendent pedicels. Not always the easiest plant to grow well, it needs a warm climate and good care; it grows especially successfully (to 8 to 12 feet) in climates that are frost free (or nearly so).

MME. ALFRED CARRIÈRE (1879)

Pinkish white. This one looks a bit different from the others of its group, betraying a probable shot of Bourbon in its ancestry. It's big and vigorous, with plentiful gray-green foliage; you can use it as a climber or maintain it as a large, arching shrub. The blush white to lightest salmon pink flowers are moderately large, full, and sweetly fragrant.

RÊVE D'OR (1869)

Golden apricot. The foliage is among the best you'll see on any climbing rose—thick, semiglossy, bronzed green. The plant is vigorous and freely branching; the fairly large, moderately full, shapely blossoms vary from buff apricot to gold to nearly orange, depending on the weather.

Rêve d'Or

TOP TO BOTTOM: Crépuscule, Jaune Desprez, Maréchal Niel, Alister Stella Gray

Lady Hillingdon (climbing form)

TEA ROSES

The first two China roses brought to Europe were 'Old Blush' and 'Slater's Crimson China' (see page 31). Some years later, two more arrived: 'Park's Yellow Tea-scented China' and 'Hume's Blush Tea-scented China'. These last two formed the foundation of the class that became known as tea roses, an extensive group often called "the aristocrats of the rose world." Where winter allows their survival (10°F/–12°C is about the limit), most build a framework of long-lived wood to become large, dense, well-foliaged shrubs that are hardly without bloom from the first spring flush until frost. Most are resistant to common foliage diseases.

The color range is largely pastel—white, cream, yellow, pink—with a few more vivid varieties; the sweetly scented blossoms are often carried on flexible pedicels that give them a graceful droop. Many of the teas show the traits that typify their descendants, the hybrid teas: long, pointed buds, informal open flowers, bushy plants that rebloom reliably throughout the growing season.

You can prune teas to restrict their size somewhat, but as a group they do not like hard pruning and may take several years to recover from it. Most varieties easily reach a height of 4 to 6 feet; taller kinds can attain 6 to 8 feet or more.

DEVONIENSIS (1838)

Cream blend. Long, ovoid buds open to reveal a blossom packed with petals—sometimes even with a button eye—in a melting pastel mixture of cream, gold, and pink. Judging strictly from the large-thorned, upright canes and moderate amount of stiff, dark foliage, you might mistake the plant for a hybrid tea of a century later. The bush establishes slowly but eventually reaches a good size in warm climates. The climbing form is much more vigorous but produces few blooms after the spring flush.

DUCHESSE DE BRABANT (1857)

Pink. This tall, rounded, dense plant is constantly in bloom, bearing cupped, moderately full, medium pink flowers with shell-shaped petals. The sport 'Mme. Joseph Schwartz' (1880) has pink-blushed ivory flowers on an identical plant.

LADY HILLINGDON (1910)

Yellow. Decorative plum purple new growth harmonizes well with the large, moderately full, saffron yellow blossoms that open from long, pointed buds. The upright, spreading bush is tall and rather open, less dense than most other teas. A climbing sport produces the same lovely blossoms and leaves on a climber of moderate size.

MAMAN COCHET (1893)

Pink. Perfect hybrid tea–type buds of warm pink develop into very full, light pink blossoms with cream shadings.

Maman Cochet

The bush is tall and spreading. Its sport 'White Maman Cochet' (1896) has creamy ivory flowers blushed pink on the outer petals. Both the pink and the white Cochets have vigorous climbing sports.

MARIE VAN HOUTTE (1871)

Yellow and pink. Smooth foliage, bronzy when new, covers a vigorous, rounded plant bearing cupped, moderately double flowers. The blooms open creamy yellow shaded pink, but turn predominantly pink as they age.

MLLE. FRANZISKA KRÜGER (1880)

Yellow and pink. No other tea produces more flowers in a year. Shapely, pointed buds swirl open to very double blossoms whose color varies greatly with the weather—from creamy yellow with pink to golden orange with lighter tints. The vigorous plant is upright but bushy and rounded. 'Blumenschmidt' (1906) is a mostly-yellow sport.

Safrano

TOP: Marie van Houtte
BOTTOM: Mons. Tillier

MME. LAMBARD (1878)

Deep pink blend. Pointed, carmine red buds produce medium-size flowers full of rather narrow petals that combine creamy gold and warm salmon when new, then darken to carmine before they fall. The plant is upright, bushy, vigorous, and easy to grow. It is also sold as 'Mme. Lombard'.

MONS. TILLIER (1891)

Reddish pink. Also sold as 'Archiduc Joseph' (which may be its original and correct name), this is an extraordinary rose. Opening from plump red buds, the flat, circular blossoms are packed with petals in old-rose style—but in shades of warm dark pink with gold, brick red, and lilac tints. Lustrous, diseaseproof, almost hollylike foliage completely covers a tall, rounded, thorny bush that can be planted as a barrier hedge.

MRS. DUDLEY CROSS (1907)

Cream, gold, and pink. The plump buds are creamy gold with pink on the petal margins; the open blossoms are camellialike, with row upon row of symmetrical petals that are gold in the blossom's center, paling to creamy white. The bush is large, rounded, and broadly vase shaped, with stiff stems and large, diseaseproof leaves.

SAFRANO (1839)

Buff and gold. Pointed, tannish orange buds that mimic perfect hybrid tea style quickly open to informal blossoms that change from gold to buff to creamy beige before the petals fall. The plant is a large, wide-angled, rounded bush, always in bloom. New growth has a bronzy plum color.

Hybrid Perpetual Roses

If the teas can be said to embody refinement, the hybrid perpetuals certainly have staked out opulence for their own. In 19th-century rose development, they were the logical next step beyond the Portland and Bourbon types. Their ancestries include China and 'Autumn Damask'—enough to ensure repeat flowering—as well as gallica, damask, and centifolia to influence floral style, fragrance, and plant and foliage character.

Capacity for repeat flowering varies from variety to variety, though none is as prolific after the spring flush as a China or tea. This more sporadic bloom, however, is a tradeoff for greater hardiness and guaranteed vigor in colder-winter regions. In the 19th century, hybrid perpetuals were the roses most likely to succeed in northern Europe and in colder parts of the United States, as long as they received some winter protection. Most are large plants (typically to 4 to 6 feet, often taller), and many are a bit coarse—but when the blooms are this sumptuous, who cares? Many send out rangy or arching canes that can be pegged down or spread out as you would do for a climber; either sort of training encourages greater bloom.

AMERICAN BEAUTY (1875)

Light red. In France, its original name was 'Mme. Ferdinand Jamain', but when renamed 'American Beauty' in the United States (surely one of the shrewder 19th-century marketing decisions!), it achieved runaway popularity as a florist's rose. Fat, ovoid buds on long, strong stems open to strongly scented, full-petaled, globular flowers of smoky dark pink to light crimson. The smaller-flowered 'Climbing American Beauty' is not a sport of this rose but one of its offspring; it blooms only in spring.

BARONESS ROTHSCHILD (1868)

Pink. This rose has much in common with the Portlands. It's an upright, bushy plant with gray-green foliage that continues up the stem to embrace the flowers—medium-size, full, shallow cups of symmetrically arranged petals in clear rose pink. 'Mabel Morrison' (1878) is a blush white sport.

BARON GIROD DE L'AIN (1897)

Red and white. A sport of 'Eugène Fürst' (1875), this rose has the same velvety deep crimson blossoms with reflexed outer petals and cupped inner ones; what sets it apart is the thin border of white on each petal. Fragrant flowers appear in small clusters on a vigorous plant thickly clothed with large leaves.

BARONNE PRÉVOST (1842)

Pink. The full, bright rose pink blossoms look like a larger version of typical Portland blooms. Cupped to flat or slightly recurved, they usually have a central buttonlike eye. The upright bush has thorny stems and somewhat coarse leaves; it flowers more heavily than most varieties in the class.

FRAU KARL DRUSCHKI (1901)

Frau Karl Druschki

White. Long, pointed buds, sometimes tinged pink, always unfurl to full, sparkling white blossoms that open completely even in damp regions. An extremely vigorous plant with long, arching canes, it can be trained as a restrained climber, though a truly climbing sport is also available.

GÉNÉRAL JACQUEMINOT (1853)

Red. This is the historic "Jack rose," an ancestor of virtually all contemporary red hybrid teas. Full, slightly cupped, highly fragrant blossoms of cherry crimson open from shapely darker red buds. The plant is strong and upright.

HENRY NEVARD (1924)

Red. Glowing deep crimson blossoms—large, cupped, and strongly fragrant—are perfectly complemented by ample dark green foliage on a husky, upright bush to about 5 feet.

HUGH DICKSON (1905)

Red. A stalwart plant that, when well grown, prefers to be a modest climber rather than a tidy bush — and in fact, it flowers more profusely when trained as a climber. The large, full, fragrant flowers are cup shaped, cherry crimson to dark red, often produced in clusters at the ends of long canes.

LA REINE (1842)

Pink. Compared to its large and lusty companions, this rose is almost demure. Very full, cupped, medium pink flowers are freely produced on a bushy plant to about 3 feet high.

MRS. JOHN LAING (1887)

Pink. Plump but shapely buds with curled-back petal edges open to full, rather cupped, fragrant flowers on strong stems. The bush is tall and vigorous (but not rangy), with small thorns and light green foliage.

PAUL NEYRON (1869)

Deep pink. Though the nickname "cabbage rose" is usually applied to centifolias, the term is just as appropriate for this individual: its fat buds unfold to huge blossoms loaded with row upon row of petals in a deep, slightly bluish pink. The bush is tall, somewhat arching, and nearly thornless, with lettuce green leaves.

PRINCE CAMILLE DE ROHAN (1861)

Dark red. Full, medium-size, powerfully fragrant blossoms have velvety petals that display a variety of dark tones, from maroon to nearly black. This rose rewards extra care with

Général Jacqueminot

greater vigor and beauty, forming an arching, bushy plant to about 4 feet high.

REINE DES VIOLETTES (1860)

Magenta violet. Aside from its repeat-flowering ability, this one has much more in common with gallicas than with other hybrid perpetuals. Full, flat flowers with a central button eye start out carmine red, then quickly fade to shades of magenta, violet, and lavender. The medium-tall plant is nearly thornless, with gray-green leaves.

ROGER LAMBELIN (1890)

Red and white. A sport of 'Prince Camille de Rohan', this rose offers the same velvety dark purplish red color—but its wavy-edged petals are precisely margined in white. The heavily fragrant blossoms are at their best when you pay special attention to fertilizing and watering.

SOUVENIR DU DOCTEUR JAMAIN (1865)

Dark red. Strong perfume and strong color combine in this sumptuous blossom. Black-shaded petals the color of port wine compose a cupped, ruffled-looking flower. With attentive watering and fertilizing, the arching plant grows large enough to serve as a small climber.

ULRICH BRUNNER FILS (1881)

Light red. This tall, slender, nearly thornless plant bears great cup-shaped, intensely fragrant blossoms of carmine pink to light crimson. As is true for most long-caned hybrid perpetuals, the canes can be splayed out or pegged down to get more bloom from flowering laterals.

TOP: Paul Neyron
BOTTOM: Reine des Violettes

HYBRID TEAS
AND
GRANDIFLORAS

To gardeners and nongardeners alike, the word "rose" brings to mind a long, stylish bud on a long, leafy stem. Indeed, it is these sorts of roses—the hybrid teas and grandifloras—that are mass-marketed every year in nurseries, garden centers, and glossy color catalogs. In the never-ending pursuit for the perfect rose blossom, they constitute the best of the quest.

For the home grower, the hybrid teas and grandifloras are flower factories, bountiful providers of a rainbow of garden colors as well as beautiful blooms for cutting. Hybrid teas typically carry one blossom at the end of each flowering stem; they bloom profusely in spring, then continue to produce blossoms until chill, frosty weather puts an end to new growth. Grandifloras have much in common with hybrid teas (including bloom time), but their typically larger bushes feature small clusters of blossoms as well as individual blooms; flower size may be equal to or a bit smaller than that of the average hybrid tea.

In the following pages, plants described as short (or low growing) are under 3 feet high; medium growers are around 4 feet, while tall types reach 5 feet or more.

Modern hybrid teas and grandifloras (and, in this public garden, a few floribundas
for good measure) represent the latest in flower color, shape, and longevity.

Brandy

The letters AARS at the end of an entry indicate that the rose has received the All-America Rose Selection Award (see page 123). For some roses, an alternate name is noted in parentheses. This may be the name by which the variety is known in other countries, or it may be an incorrect name under which it is sometimes marketed.

AMERICAN SPIRIT (hybrid tea; 1988)

Bright red. Long, pointed, dark red buds open to large, full blossoms of unchanging bright red, with petals that look like velvet; flowers are equally attractive in both warm and cool climates. The plant is tall, with dark green, glossy foliage.

ARIZONA (grandiflora; 1975)

Copper orange. Urn-shaped buds open to glowing gold-tinted orange flowers that stand out against the dark, coppery green leaves. The tall, extra-vigorous bush is good as a specimen shrub; a number of plants set out in a row can serve as a tall hedge. AARS 1975.

ARLENE FRANCIS (hybrid tea; 1957)

Golden yellow. Long, pointed buds of beautiful form open to large, moderately full flowers with a powerful fragrance. The somewhat spreading bush reaches medium height and is mantled in glossy dark green leaves.

ARTISTRY (hybrid tea; 1996)

Coral orange. From the plump, pointed buds to the broad-petaled open blossoms, the color—a soft coral orange—remains largely unchanged. A husky, medium-tall bush with plenty of large, glossy leaves completes the picture. AARS 1997.

BARBARA BUSH (hybrid tea; 1991)

Pink and cream. An offspring of 'Pristine', this rose has its parent's finest qualities—plus more color in the blossoms. Ovoid buds open to full, creamy white blooms blushed and overlaid with coral pink, the color growing more intense at the petal edges and as the flowers age. The plant is fairly tall, with dark green leaves.

BEWITCHED (hybrid tea; 1967)

Medium rose pink. Long, stylish-looking buds on long, strong stems open slowly to fragrant "show rose" flowers in rose pink with paler petal backs. Healthy gray-green foliage clothes the tall, compact plant. AARS 1967.

BLUE GIRL (Kölner Karnival) (hybrid tea; 1964)

Lavender. Shapely buds of silvery deep lilac open to full, cup-shaped flowers with a potent fragrance; cool weather produces the best blooms. The bushy, somewhat spreading plant reaches medium height and boasts dark, glossy, notably disease-resistant foliage. For the climbing form, see page 77.

BRANDY (hybrid tea; 1981)

Golden apricot. The glowing golden amber color explains the name. Unfurling from burnt orange buds, the large, broad-petaled, mildly fragrant flowers open well in all kinds of weather. Dark green leaves (bronzy when new) complement the blossoms; the plant is upright and medium-tall. AARS 1982.

BRIGADOON (hybrid tea; 1991)

Warm pink blend. From bud to open flower, the delicious combination of strawberry and cream constantly changes: pink-blushed, pointed buds unfold to camellialike, warm dark pink blossoms with creamy recesses. The bush is tall and slightly spreading, clothed in healthy dark green foliage. AARS 1992.

BROADWAY (hybrid tea; 1986)

Pink and yellow blend. Urn-shaped buds are golden orange suffused with pink; as they unfold, the pink tones increase and intensify at the petal edges, while the gold shades lighten to yellow. The tall, strong plant has leathery dark green leaves.

CAMELOT (grandiflora; 1964)

Coral pink. Medium-size, coral pink blossoms, very full and fragrant, open from ovoid buds that usually come in clusters. Productivity and general health are noteworthy; the tall, slightly spreading plant has nearly diseaseproof foliage. AARS 1965.

CARIBBEAN (grandiflora; 1992)

Orange and yellow blend. Full, pointed buds in a blend of tangerine and gold spiral open to softer-toned flowers with pointed petal tips. Long stems bear blooms both individually and in small clusters; the bush is vigorous and upright growing, with bright green leaves. AARS 1994.

CARY GRANT (hybrid tea; 1987)

Orange and red blend. The name lets you know that this rose has class. Long, tapered buds are a vivid reddish orange, washed yellow at the bases; the large, full, shapely, fragrant flowers are orange with a red overlay. The plant is medium-tall and upright.

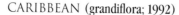
Caribbean

CHICAGO PEACE (hybrid tea; 1962)

Pink and gold blend. A color sport of 'Peace', this has the same virtues in foliage, plant, and magnificent flower form—but its blooms come in a livelier color blend of bronzy orange-yellow and deep pink. The strong, spreading, medium-size bush is outfitted in quilted, leathery leaves.

CHRISTIAN DIOR (hybrid tea; 1958)

Cherry red. Borne on a tall and rather upright bush, elegant blood-red buds unfurl to unscented blooms of a slightly lighter red, a bit paler and duller on the petal backs. Flowers remain attractive when fully open and do not fade or turn bluish. AARS 1962.

CHRISTOPHER COLUMBUS (hybrid tea; 1991)

Orange and red blend. Vibrant tropical colors make this rose a focal point in the garden. Ovoid orange-red buds, brushed red at the margins, unfurl to full, bright orange blossoms that retain the red petal edges. These vivid flowers are backed by plentiful dark green foliage on a plant of medium height.

CHRYSLER IMPERIAL (hybrid tea; 1952)

Deep crimson. A classic rose with shapely buds, full blossoms, and a rich fragrance; the velvety dark red flowers turn purplish red as they age. Bushy, free-flowering plants of medium height have dark green, rather dull foliage. AARS 1953.

COLOR MAGIC (hybrid tea; 1978)

Pink blend. The magic is in the change of colors: creamy pink buds open to large, fragrant, ivory-centered flowers that are suffused with deep reddish pink as they age. The medium-tall, upright bush has unusually large leaves. AARS 1978.

Color Magic

TOP: Camelot
MIDDLE: Broadway
BOTTOM: Cary Grant

CRYSTALLINE (hybrid tea; 1987)

Pure white. Once a greenhouse rose grown for cut flowers, this variety has "escaped" to the garden, where it provides long-stemmed flowers with the elegance of fine crystal. Both the tapered, pointed buds and the full, shapely flowers are stark white, carried on a tall, upright bush cloaked in dark green leaves.

DAINTY BESS (hybrid tea; 1925)

Rose pink. Perfect single blossoms of delicate rose pink are centered with contrasting maroon stamens. The graceful, 3- to 4-inch, five-petaled blooms are typically borne in small clusters; the plant is upright and medium-tall.

DESERT PEACE (hybrid tea; 1992)

Yellow and red blend. Imagine a 'Peace' rose with intensified color, and you'll have an idea of this 'Peace' descendant's looks: cream to golden yellow petals are shaded apricot, their margins brushed with red to deep pink. Buds are more slender and pointed than those of 'Peace', the flowers not as full. Plants are upright and medium-tall.

Dainty Bess

DOLLY PARTON (hybrid tea; 1984)

Orange red. Both the large, pointed, ovoid buds and full, intensely fragrant blossoms are glowing orange red. Medium-tall, spreading bushes have large, dark leaves that are somewhat susceptible to mildew.

DOUBLE DELIGHT (hybrid tea; 1977)

White and red. Unmistakable blooms feature camellialike form and petals of creamy white brushed red on the edges; the amount of red varies with the weather (there's more in heat and sun) and spreads over more of the petal surfaces as flowers age. The spreading, glossy-leafed bush grows to medium height. AARS 1977.

ELINA (hybrid tea; 1983)

Pale yellow. Its perfect form—from the smartly tapered buds to the camellialike open blossoms—and luminous cream to light yellow color make this rose a delight to the eye. The healthy, vigorous, dark-foliaged, medium-tall plant succeeds in virtually all rose-growing regions.

FAME! (grandiflora; 1998)

Deep pink. Here's a rival to 'Miss All-American Beauty' in the electric pink category. The large, ovoid buds open to camellialike blossoms of a dark shocking pink—a color impossible to ignore. The plant is tall, bushy, and extremely robust, with plenty of dark green leaves. AARS 1998.

FIRST PRIZE (hybrid tea; 1970)

Deep pink. Fabulous, very long, spiral buds of deep pink unfold to really large flowers that are distinctly lighter at the center. Vigorous, medium-size, spreading bushes bear attractive dark green foliage that is somewhat susceptible to mildew.

FOUNTAIN SQUARE (hybrid tea; 1986)

White. A sport of 'Pristine', this rose has the elegant buds and shapely flowers of its parent—but the blossom color is a pure, truly pristine white. The upright-growing, medium-tall plant produces good cutting stems with dark green foliage.

Dolly Parton

Double Delight

First Prize

Fragrant Cloud

Gold Medal

FRAGRANT CLOUD (hybrid tea; 1963)

Coral orange. Long, scarlet-orange buds open to moderately full, somewhat paler flowers with an intense and delightful fragrance. Profusely flowering, bushy plants of medium height are clothed in glossy dark green leaves.

FRAGRANT MEMORY (Jadis) (hybrid tea; 1974)

Rose pink. Powerful fragrance and beautiful form are the hallmarks of this heavy-blooming, clear pink rose. Slender, urn-shaped buds produce moderately full flowers of an intense, even color. The plant is tall and slender.

FRENCH PERFUME (hybrid tea; 1994)

Yellow, cream, and pink blend. Pointed yellow buds with pink on the outer petals soften to creamy yellow with increasing pink flushes as they unfold; fully open blossoms are creamy white and pinkish red. The perfume is strong and fruity. The medium-tall plant has dark foliage.

GARDEN PARTY (hybrid tea; 1959)

Ivory and pink. Long, tapered ivory buds are tinted pink on the petal edges, the pink tones suffusing more of the petal surface as the buds open to ruffled, stiffly perfect blossoms. The medium-size, spreading plant has matte foliage that is susceptible to mildew. AARS 1960.

GOLDEN MASTERPIECE (hybrid tea; 1954)

Deep yellow. Long, large buds expand into some of the largest blooms among roses—and the full, fragrant flowers hold their color well. Strong-growing plants are upright and bushy, outfitted in dark, highly glossy foliage.

GOLD MEDAL (grandiflora; 1982)

Golden yellow. Great vigor and good health are among this rose's winning traits. Small clusters of long, ovoid, golden yellow buds—sometimes tinged with pink or orange—unfurl to large, full, fragrant blossoms. The plant is very tall and upright.

GREAT CENTURY (Grand Siècle) (hybrid tea; 1987)

Pink and cream blend. The smoothly blended opalescent colors are presented in huge, breathtaking blossoms with the shape and symmetry of camellias; in cool weather, fully open flowers can reach 8 inches across. The spreading bush grows to medium height.

HEIRLOOM (hybrid tea; 1972)

Magenta blend. Ovoid, deep lilac to purple buds open to full, deliciously fragrant flowers of a rich lilac magenta—a color not seen in any other modern hybrid tea. Dark green leaves clothe the medium-tall bush.

HELMUT SCHMIDT (hybrid tea; 1979)

Medium yellow. Exhibition-quality flowers make this one a frequent award-winner at rose society shows. The buds are long and pointed, the long-stemmed blossoms sweet scented and moderately full. Matte gray-green leaves clothe an upright bush that reaches medium height.

HONOR (hybrid tea; 1980)

Pure white. Long, pointed, satiny white buds slowly unfurl to really large, long-lasting blossoms; the flowers are only moderately full. Leathery-textured, olive green leaves cover a tall, upright plant. AARS 1980.

Honor

Just Joey

John F. Kennedy

La France

INGRID BERGMAN (hybrid tea; 1985)

Deep red. From the shapely, ovoid buds to the full-petaled open flowers, the color remains the same: a solid, rich red with no fading or bluing. Bushy plants are of medium height or a bit shorter, cloaked in dark green, semiglossy leaves with good disease resistance.

JOHN F. KENNEDY (hybrid tea; 1965)

Pure white. Long, classically tapered buds (often tinged with green) slowly spiral open to form full, notably fragrant, pristine blossoms of great size. Flowers have the best form in warm regions. The medium-tall plant has dark, leathery foliage.

JUST JOEY (hybrid tea; 1972)

Buff orange. Here's a pleasing medley of soft, warm tones. From attractive buff-orange buds come moderately full, highly fragrant flowers that soften to apricot shades. Large, glossy leaves adorn a bushy, upright plant of medium height.

KING'S RANSOM (hybrid tea; 1961)

Deep yellow. Long buds of classic hybrid tea shape open to large, full flowers with an unfading chrome yellow color and a pronounced sweet scent. The upright, medium-tall bush bears dark, glossy leaves. AARS 1962.

KORDES PERFECTA (hybrid tea; 1957)

Cream and pink. Pointed buds of pink-edged cream are huge and flawless; when conditions are right, they spiral open to breathtaking fully double flowers. This rose does best with a bit of shade (especially in hot-summer regions) and less fertilizer than other hybrid teas appreciate. The tall, vigorous, upright bush has dark green leaves (bronzy when new)

LA FRANCE (hybrid tea; 1867)

Rose pink. The first rose to be designated a hybrid tea (see page 10), this one is not only historic but lovely as well. From plump buds come very double blossoms with rolled-back petal margins; petal backs are a bit darker than the upper surfaces. The overall impression is of an old-style flower on a modern, bushy plant of about medium height. (An imposter also circulates under the name 'La France'; it is recognizable by its more slender and pointed buds, lighter and warmer pink color, and taller and more rangy plant.)

LAGERFELD (grandiflora; 1986)

Lavender. Medium-size, pointed buds of classic hybrid tea shape swirl open to form subtly elegant blossoms in shimmering, silvery lavender. These long-stemmed flowers are carried in small clusters on a vigorous, tall-growing bush with matte medium green foliage.

LOVE (grandiflora; 1980)

Red and white. Brilliant red petals with silvery white backs unfold from beautifully pointed buds; half-open blooms show a combination of red and white, while fully open ones look entirely red. The medium-size plant has a somewhat spreading habit. AARS 1980.

MAGIC LANTERN (grandiflora; 1989)

Orange blend. This Hungarian beauty brings the colors of a glowing fire to the garden. Its ovoid buds open to good-sized coppery golden orange blossoms with a pleasing light fragrance. The plant is medium-tall and upright.

MEDALLION (hybrid tea; 1973)

Light buff orange. Everything about this rose is large, from the extra-long buds to the open flowers to the plant itself. Buff apricot verging on orange in bud, the licorice-scented blossoms turn slightly paler and take on pink tones as they open. The tall, spreading plant has dark foliage. AARS 1973.

MIDAS TOUCH (hybrid tea; 1992)

Bright yellow. Blooms of an unshaded brilliant yellow glow like beacons in the garden. Pointed buds open to moderately full flowers with jauntily waved petal edges; the blossoms hold their color until the petals fall. The medium-size plant has dark, semiglossy foliage. AARS 1994.

MIKADO (hybrid tea; 1988)

Cherry red. A touch of yellow at each petal base enhances the bright cherry color. Urn-shaped, flat-topped buds unfold to full, unfading blossoms with a light fragrance. The plant is of moderate size, covered with highly glossy leaves. AARS 1988.

Medallion

MIRANDY (hybrid tea; 1945)

Dark red. Full, intensely fragrant flowers of velvety dark red open from plump, pointed, ovoid buds. Performance is outstanding in warm, humid regions, but blooms tend to "ball" and turn purple where weather is cool and foggy. The plant is very bushy and reaches medium height. AARS 1945.

MISS ALL-AMERICAN BEAUTY (Maria Callas). (hybrid tea; 1965)

Cerise. A big, bold blossom in a color you can't overlook: something between a deep shocking pink and a light red. Ovoid buds and very full, well-formed flowers come on a leathery-leafed, husky, somewhat spreading plant of medium height. AARS 1968.

TOP: Love
MIDDLE: Midas Touch
BOTTOM: Miss All-American Beauty

Mister Lincoln

Mon Cheri

Oklahoma

MISTER LINCOLN (hybrid tea; 1964)

Rich red. A completely satisfactory and satisfying rich red for all regions. Long, lovely buds open to very full, long-stemmed flowers with a powerful fragrance. The tall, strong-growing plant has dark, glossy foliage. AARS 1965.

MON CHERI (hybrid tea; 1981)

Pink to red. The combination of vivid pink and glowing red is almost too bright to look at. Soft pink buds open to very full blossoms that turn velvety red wherever sun strikes the petals. Dark green foliage clothes the medium-size bush. AARS 1982.

MONTEZUMA (grandiflora; 1955)

Red and coral blend. Beautifully formed buds grow lighter as they open, turning from nearly red to coral salmon (or coral orange in warm weather). Flowers are particularly long lasting, both on the bush and when cut. The plant is robust, tall, and slightly spreading, with leathery, disease-resistant foliage.

MOON SHADOW (hybrid tea; 1996)

Lavender. Neither silver nor purple, this one occupies a special niche among the small group of mauve roses: the color is a dusky, shadowy lavender. The blossoms are full, shapely, and intensely fragrant, borne on a vigorous, medium-size bush with glossy foliage.

MT. HOOD (grandiflora; 1991)

Ivory white. With this name, what other color could it be but white? Clusters of pointed buds open to full-petaled, fragrant, 3-inch blossoms, plentifully produced on an upright, medium-tall, much-branched bush outfitted in healthy, glossy dark green leaves. AARS 1996.

NEW DAY (hybrid tea; 1977)

Soft yellow. Classically long, tapered buds and clear, unshaded color make this spicy-scented, free-blooming yellow rose a favorite. Leathery gray-green foliage clothes an upright, fairly thorny plant of medium height.

NEW YEAR (grandiflora; 1983)

Orange and gold blend. On the short side (medium height) for a grandiflora, but no less vigorous or productive than the usual representative of the class. Dark green, glossy leaves provide a handsome backdrop for a profusion of bright gold-orange buds and well-formed blossoms in a softer orange. AARS 1987.

OKLAHOMA (hybrid tea; 1964)

Black red. Inky black buds open to very large, rather globular, dusky red blooms that remain beautiful when fully open; an intense perfume adds to the appeal. The plant is a lusty grower, but the flowers are not at their best in cool, foggy regions.

New Year

OLDTIMER (hybrid tea; 1969)

🌹 Bronzed golden apricot. Very large, elegant blossoms with satiny-textured petals develop from long, streamlined buds. Color is a golden apricot with tints of bronze or copper. The bush is tall and upright, with leathery, pointed leaves.

OLÉ (grandiflora; 1964)

🌹 Red orange. Very full, ruffled and frilled blooms of blinding red orange could almost be mistaken for tuberous begonias or oversize carnations. The bushy, vigorous, medium-size plant has dark hollylike leaves.

OLYMPIAD (hybrid tea; 1984)

🌹 Bright red. Tall, upright plant produces brilliant red blossoms on cutting-length stems. Long buds open to large, long-lasting, lightly scented flowers that hold their color without turning bluish. Foliage is grayish green and healthy. AARS 1984.

OPENING NIGHT (hybrid tea; 1998)

🌹 Rich red. This worthy offspring of 'Olympiad' has inherited the parent's overall vigor, long stems, and perfect form (from bud to open blossom)—but the long-lasting blooms have an even richer color. Dark green leaves clothe a medium-tall bush. AARS 1998.

OREGOLD (hybrid tea; 1975)

🌹 Saffron yellow. A tawny tint adds extra richness to this rose's basic deep golden yellow hue. Long, pointed buds open to full, shapely, lightly scented blossoms in a softer yellow. Dark, glossy leaves clothe an upright, medium-size bush. AARS 1975.

PARADISE (hybrid tea; 1978)

🌹 Lavender and red. Here is a distinctive color combination: silvery lavender petals
🌹 are edged in ruby red, with the red tones spreading over more of the petal surfaces as the flowers age. Shapely buds open to moderately full flowers on a husky, medium-size plant with leathery dark green leaves. AARS 1979.

PASCALI (hybrid tea; 1963)

🌹 Warm white. Perhaps the finest white rose for dependable production of good-quality flowers in all climates. Tapered, pointed buds unfold to full, perfectly formed, medium-size blossoms with a light perfume. The tall, upright, dark-foliaged plant is especially free flowering. AARS 1969.

PEACE (hybrid tea; 1945)

🌹 Yellow and pink blend. So well known it hardly needs a description. Full, ovoid
🌹 buds of yellow touched with pink or red slowly unfold into glorious, extra-large blossoms with pink-rimmed yellow petals. The strong-growing, large-caned, spreading bush reaches medium height and has large, glossy leaves. AARS 1946.

PERFECT MOMENT (hybrid tea; 1991)

🌹 Yellow and red blend. Each plant of this rose should come with a complimentary
🌹 pair of dark glasses! The plump, rather urn-shaped buds are bright yellow brushed with red; as the full flowers slowly unfurl, you see a yellow interior blending out to a broad, bright red margin. The upright, medium-size plant has dark green leaves. AARS 1991.

TOP TO BOTTOM: Oregold, Paradise, Peace, Perfect Moment

PERFUME DELIGHT (hybrid tea; 1973)

Deep pink. Rich, spicy fragrance is one asset, and another is the bud and flower form: flawless long, spiral buds unfurl to perfect 5-inch flowers of satiny deep pink. The medium-size bush is compact and upright, with large, dark leaves. AARS 1974.

PINK PEACE (hybrid tea; 1959)

Deep rose. Not really a pink duplicate of 'Peace', yet it too produces numerous large, full, shapely blooms from plump, ovoid buds. The heady fragrance is a bonus. The upright bush grows to medium height, bearing leathery, dark green leaves that are susceptible to rust.

PRINCESSE DE MONACO (hybrid tea; 1981)

Cream and pink. Dainty pastel colors mingle in a large blossom that is full, yet graceful. Plump, creamy yellow buds with pinkish red margins slowly open to ivory-petaled blooms with a wider edge of cherry pink. The medium-low, upright-growing bush has glossy foliage.

PRISTINE (hybrid tea; 1978)

Blush white. Too pink to be really white, but too white to be classed as a pink, this delicate confection of a blossom comes on a plant that is anything but delicate: medium-tall and spreading, with oversize dark green leaves. Long, ovoid, pink-blushed buds quickly open to full, long-lasting, pink-tinted ivory blooms with a light fragrance.

PROUD LAND (hybrid tea; 1969)

Bright red. Full-petaled, velvety bright red blossoms offer a heavy, pervasive perfume. The buds are long, pointed, and freely produced on long stems; the upright plant reaches medium height.

QUEEN ELIZABETH (grandiflora; 1954)

Clear pink. The first rose to be designated "grandiflora," it set the class standard for vigor and productivity. Small clusters of radiant pink, medium-size blooms develop from attractive pointed buds; the tall, extremely vigorous plant is clothed in dark, glossy foliage. For all practical purposes, this is a shrub rose, suitable for hedges and background planting. AARS 1955.

RIO SAMBA (hybrid tea; 1991)

Yellow and red blend. Pointed buds and moderately full open flowers are a bit small for a hybrid tea, but the color makes up for the size: molten gold petals are brushed and tipped in brightest red orange. Blooms come both singly and in small clusters on a bushy, dark-foliaged plant of medium height. AARS 1993.

TOP LEFT: Perfume Delight   TOP RIGHT: Princesse de Monaco
MIDDLE: Pristine
BOTTOM: Rio Samba

ROYAL HIGHNESS
(hybrid tea; 1962)

🌹 Palest pink. The porcelain-like blush pink buds and regal flowers are of the highest quality. Long, pointed buds slowly unfold to magnificent full, sweetly fragrant blossoms. Dark green, glossy leaves adorn a medium-tall, upright bush. AARS 1963.

SAINT PATRICK
(hybrid tea; 1995)

🌹 Greenish yellow. Compare a bud of this rose with that of any other yellow and you'll immediately understand the name: the color is plainly chartreuse. These shapely buds slowly spiral open to golden yellow blooms in cool weather, yellow-green ones when it's hot. Gray-green foliage clothes the medium-size plant. AARS 1996.

Saint Patrick

SEASHELL (hybrid tea; 1976)

🌹 Salmon pink. Deep apricot buds unfold to very full, fragrant blossoms in rich tones of salmon pink to light orange, with shadings of yellow and cream. Dark green leaves clothe an upright, medium-size, heavy-blooming bush.

SECRET (hybrid tea; 1992)

🌹 Cream and pink blend. The secret is a memorable, sweet-spicy perfume. Lovely pointed, oval buds are a pastel medley of cream, white, and pink; they unfurl to full, shapely blossoms in which the darkest pink tones are brushed on petal margins. Plum-brown new leaves mature to a semi-glossy dark green, carried on a bush of medium height. AARS 1994.

SHEER BLISS (hybrid tea; 1987)

🌹 Cream and pink. Long, ovoid buds of a luscious creamy white lightly blushed with pink open to full, fragrant flowers with darker pink centers. Dark, glossy foliage clothes an upright plant of medium height. AARS 1987.

SHEER ELEGANCE (hybrid tea; 1989)

🌹 Pink and cream blend. Elegant indeed is this confection of peach and cream with hints of gold. Tapered buds expand to full, lightly scented blossoms—creamy in the center, growing pinker toward the petal margins. The upright, medium-size bush is outfitted in glossy dark green leaves. AARS 1991.

SHREVEPORT (grandiflora; 1981)

🌹 Orange blend. The artistic combination of colors—orange, salmon, coral, and yellow—gives an overall impression of soft orange. Shapely buds and full, medium-size flowers usually come one to a stem on tall, strong-growing plants. AARS 1982.

SIGNATURE (hybrid tea; 1996)

🌹 Deep pink. Satiny petals with pointed tips give this flower the look of a ribbon rose on a truly grand scale. Elegant red buds unfurl to blossoms of a deep, glowing pink, the petal backs brushed cream in their lower half to create a subtle bicolor effect. Vigorous, medium-tall plants are decked out in leathery dark green leaves.

TOP LEFT: Sheer Bliss   TOP RIGHT: Secret   BOTTOM: Shreveport

TOP TO BOTTOM: Solitude, Sonia (LEFT),
Sunbright(RIGHT), Sunset Celebration,
Sweet Surrender

SNOWFIRE (hybrid tea; 1970)

Red and white. The name describes the colors: brilliant, velvety red petals with white backs. The ovoid buds are white, revealing more and more red as they open to large, lightly fragrant blossoms. The upright, thorny plant grows to medium height, bearing handsome leaves of a glossy dark green.

SOLITUDE (grandiflora; 1991)

Coral and orange blend. Despite a somber-sounding name, this is a bright, vibrant rose. Fully double blooms with lightly scalloped petal margins open from plump buds that show golden highlights on petal backs. A vigorous, medium-tall plant produces plenty of these lightly fragrant, large flowers in small clusters. AARS 1993.

SONIA (grandiflora; 1974)

Coral pink. This lovely rose began its career as a greenhouse cut-flower variety, but its beauty and good performance have assured it a place in gardens as well. It's noted for its medium-size, perfectly formed buds and fragrant, long-lasting, full, shapely flowers of soft to deep coral pink. The plant is upright and medium-tall, with dark, glossy leaves.

STAINLESS STEEL (hybrid tea; 1996)

Lavender. It's a descendant of 'Sterling Silver'—but despite its more workaday name, this rose is no less classy than its predecessor! A tall, upright, vigorous plant with large, dark leaves bears elegantly tapered, silvery lavender buds that unfold to large, moderately full flowers with a noteworthy perfume.

STERLING SILVER (hybrid tea; 1957)

Lavender. The rose that pushed lavenders into popularity, 'Sterling Silver' is still notable for its clear, silvery lavender color and intense old-rose scent. Attractive pointed buds and cup-shaped open blooms come on a medium-size, moderately vigorous bush.

SUNBRIGHT (hybrid tea; 1984)

Deep yellow. Long, urn-shaped, dark yellow buds open to large, moderately full flowers that hold their color well. The tall, robust plant blooms continuously, its bright blossoms backed by glossy dark green leaves.

SUN GODDESS (hybrid tea; 1994)

Deep yellow. Among deep yellow hybrid teas, this one is unsurpassed for vigor and good health. Tall bushes with dark green foliage produce long, pointed buds of an intense golden yellow; these spiral open to classic hybrid tea blossoms with pointed petal tips.

SUNSET CELEBRATION (hybrid tea; 1998)

Orange blend. This festival of sunset tones celebrates the centennial of *Sunset* magazine. Cream, apricot, amber, and orange mingle in shapely, full flowers that open from long, tapered buds. The plant is upright growing, of medium height. AARS 1998.

SWEET SURRENDER (hybrid tea; 1983)

Silvery pink. The heady perfume gave this rose its name. Pointed buds on long stems unfold to very full, large, silvery pink blossoms of old-rose charm. Upright bushes reach medium height. AARS 1983.

TABOO (hybrid tea; 1988)

Black red. Petals of such velvety darkness are no novelty among bearded irises—but among roses, 'Taboo' has little company. The tapered ovoid buds swirl open to moderately full blossoms in alluring, mysterious tones of red, maroon, and black. These long-stemmed novelties bloom on a medium-tall bush with dark green leaves.

TIFFANY (hybrid tea; 1954)

Warm pink. Large, long buds, as perfect as finely cut jewels, open to moderately full, warm pink blossoms with an intense, fruity fragrance. The tall, upright plant has matte dark green foliage. AARS 1955.

TIMELESS (hybrid tea; 1996)

Deep pink. This rose is undeniably beautiful—but it has more than beauty to recommend it. The long, tapered buds are slow to open; the large, moderately full blossoms are long lasting and hold their vibrant, even pink color from start to finish. Dark green leaves clothe a somewhat spreading bush of medium height. AARS 1997.

TORO (Uncle Joe) (hybrid tea; 1971)

Dark red. "Big" is the word for this robust dark red. Long, pointed, ovoid buds on long stems open slowly to large, full, shapely, moderately fragrant blossoms. Flowers open best where nights are warm. The plant is tall and upright, with dark, leathery leaves.

TOUCH OF CLASS (hybrid tea; 1984)

Warm pink blend. Heavy-petaled, long-lasting blooms shade from coral and cream to a vibrant warm pink. Large, moderately full, lightly fragrant flowers open from tapered buds. The tall, upright-growing bush is clothed in dark, glossy leaves. AARS 1986.

TOURNAMENT OF ROSES (grandiflora; 1988)

Warm pink blend. Both the ovoid buds and the symmetrical, camellialike open flowers display two shades of pink: dark coral on the petal backs, warm light pink on the upper surfaces. Glossy-leafed plants of medium height are noted both for their vigorous growth and for their profusion of bloom. AARS 1989.

TROPICANA (hybrid tea; 1960)

Orange salmon. Forerunner of the contemporary fluorescent orange roses, 'Tropicana' features medium-size, pointed buds and full, rather cupped flowers with a sweet fragrance. The vigorous, tall, somewhat spreading plant has matte green leaves that are susceptible to mildew. AARS 1963.

Voodoo

VOODOO (hybrid tea; 1986)

Orange, yellow, and pink blend. Yellow-orange buds open to large, heavily perfumed flowers that soften in color to yellow and peach shades, then finally fade to pink. The tall, upright bush carries plenty of dark bronze-green, glossy foliage. AARS 1986.

WHITE LIGHTNIN' (grandiflora; 1980)

Creamy white. Ruffled petals give the full, citrus-scented, creamy white blossoms a distinct personality. The plant is bushy, free flowering, and—at medium height—short for a grandiflora. The leaves are bright green and glossy. AARS 1981.

Tournament of Roses

Every year, millions of gardeners plant countless flowering shrubs for the beauty of their annual bloom: lilac, forsythia, flowering quince, spiraea, India hawthorn, and oleander, to name only a few.

LANDSCAPE
ROSES

The same gardeners might be surprised to learn that a wealth of roses belong on the list, too—and most of them offer the bonus of blossoming all through the growing season.

In contrast to the familiar hybrid teas and grandifloras, the so-called landscape roses are first and foremost flowering shrubs, intended to serve as hedges, borders, and backgrounds—and, of course, to supply color. Some bear blossoms nearly as large as those of hybrid teas; some show typical hybrid tea form. But others have the floral simplicity of wild roses, while still others feature the complex opulence associated with old European sorts. The plants may be bushy, fountain-like, semiclimbing, or lax and spreading, in sizes ranging from knee-high to over 10 feet tall. Among these roses, there is no archetype of perfection; what matters is the ability to deliver the goods on plants that are as trouble-free as possible.

Mail-order catalogs provide the greatest variety of landscape roses. The plants are typically listed according to a number of classes—some officially sanctioned by rose societies, some simply convenient groupings for the cataloguers. These classes are described on the next page.

Backlighting illuminates translucent petals of the hybrid musk rose 'Cornelia' (page 61).

Iceberg (floribunda)

ENGLISH ROSES

These are the work of one English rose breeder, David Austin, who aimed to combine old European floral styles with modern colors and repeat bloom. His goal has been beautifully achieved on plants that vary considerably, from definitely shrubby types to many that can be treated as small climbers in the mild-winter regions where they reach their maximum sizes. Nearly all are susceptible to the normal range of foliage diseases. The name "English rose" is a widely used marketing label; in official classification, these roses belong to the shrub roses (see facing page). All the English roses profiled here are repeat bloomers.

FLORIBUNDA ROSES

The original floribunda varieties, produced in Denmark, were achieved by crossing hybrid teas and polyanthas (see facing page); the goal was to create plants as vigorous, bushy, and profuse in bloom as polyanthas, with the color range and flower form of hybrid teas. Today's floribundas are a complex lot of plants that range in height from about 2½ to 4 feet; most are dense, stiff, and shrubby, though some are closer in general style to hybrid teas. Some bear large clusters of single or semidouble, rather informal flowers (as did the early hybrids); many have blossoms resembling small hybrid tea blooms. And some types blur the line between hybrid tea and floribunda: their blossoms are as large as those of hybrid teas, carried in few-flowered clusters or even singly. All floribundas are repeat blooming.

GROUND COVER ROSES

Like English roses, these are officially classed as shrub roses (see facing page). They are low-growing types, with canes that spread to cover the soil to a distance of about three times the plant's height. They don't offer the uniform surface of ivy or pachysandra, but when planted roughly 8 feet apart, they'll fill in to make a lumpy or undulating carpet of color. They're particularly effective when planted on slopes or where their canes can spill over the edge of a wall. All are repeat flowering.

HYBRID MUSK ROSES

Though these roses do not have *Rosa moschata,* the musk rose, as one of their immediate parents, they do have it in their ancestry—virtually all in the class stem from one common descendant of *R. moschata.* Hybrid musks are typically vigorous, lax, repeat-blooming shrubs 4 to 8 feet high and wide, with clustered flowers in the style of many floribundas. The larger-growing ones often can be treated as small climbers in mild climates. Foliage is notably disease resistant, and most varieties perform well in partial shade as well as in full sun.

HYBRID RUGOSA ROSES

The "hybrid" part of the equation varies considerably, but the *Rosa rugosa* side of their parentage has given all these varieties toughness and distinctive foliage which, in the best members of the class, is dark green and deeply veined or corrugated. In most of these hybrids, the foliage is disease resistant, though in many varieties it can be damaged by synthetic chemical sprays. Many hybrid rugosas form the large, distinctive rugosa hips (see photo on page 18); these can start to look decorative as early as mid-summer, contrasting (or, in some cases, even clashing) with the blossoms. All are repeat flowering, though 'Hansa' blooms less steadily than the other varieties. In winter, unprotected plants are notably more cold-tolerant than are modern hybrid teas and grandifloras.

POLYANTHA ROSES

This class appeared in the 19th century, at about the same time as the hybrid teas. The first polyanthas were derived from *Rosa multiflora* (page 18) and various tea roses (and their relatives, including tea-Noisettes); the resulting hybrids were short, glossy-leafed plants that produced large clusters of inch-wide, white or pink blossoms throughout the growing season. Later hybrids show improved flower form or expanded color range (or both); like the original representatives of the polyantha class, they are repeat bloomers.

SHRUB ROSES

For many years, this official class—which includes the English and ground cover roses described on the facing page—was a repository for roses that fit into none of the other established classes. Since the 1950s, however, hybridizers have devoted increasing effort to enlarging the ranks of the shrub class. The goal is rugged, well-foliaged plants that function as shrubs in the landscape and flower profusely, in the range of colors found in modern hybrid teas. Many breeders have paid special attention to flower form; some varieties feature hybrid tea–style blossoms, while the English roses represent a nod to the past. Unless other-wise noted, shrub roses flower repeatedly from spring until frost.

SPECIES HYBRID ROSES

Some landscape roses are direct progeny of a rose species and bear a notable resemblance to that rose. In the descriptions, these are designated as hybrids of the relevant species, though in one case where ancestry is conjectural ('Complicata'), the desig-nation is simply "species hybrid." Except as noted, these roses flower only in spring.

Gertrude Jekyll (English rose)

Abraham Darby (English rose)

The letters AARS at the end of an entry indicate that the rose has received the All-America Rose Selection Award (see page 123). For some roses, an alternate name is noted in parentheses. This may be the name by which the variety is known in other countries, or it may be an incorrect name under which it is sometimes marketed.

ABRAHAM DARBY (English rose; 1985)

Apricot blend. Take your pick: spreading, arching shrub (to about 10 feet) or modest climber. Either way, you'll enjoy a fragrant bounty of large, extremely full, cupped blossoms that mingle apricot, peach, gold, and cream in an always-lovely combination. The blossoms come in small clusters, backed by leathery dark green leaves on canes with notably large thorns.

ALBA MEIDILAND (shrub; 1987)

White. The combination of dark, glossy foliage and pure white flowers gives this rose a fresh, clean look throughout the growing season. Elongated, airy sprays of small, very double blossoms appear on a dense, mounding plant to about 3 feet high and 5 feet across.

ALL THAT JAZZ (shrub; 1991)

Coral salmon. A vigorous grower to about 5 feet tall, this stiff, bushy shrub has the look of an oversize floribunda. Large clusters of vivid, nearly single blossoms are displayed against plentiful high-gloss foliage that's disease resistant. AARS 1992.

AMBER QUEEN (floribunda; 1983)

Golden apricot. This rose scores high in all categories: habit, foliage, and flowers. Clusters of plump buds open to full, ruffly, scented blossoms of amber to apricot gold. Dark, bronze-tinted, almost quilted-looking foliage clothes a bushy plant about 3 feet tall. AARS 1988.

AMBRIDGE ROSE (English rose; 1990)

Apricot blend. Modern color and old-fashioned charm combine in a bushy, free-flowering, dark-foliaged plant to about 3 feet tall. The plump buds open to cupped, porcelainlike blossoms that shade from peachy apricot in the rosettelike center to pink at the edges; as the blossoms expand, the outer petals reflex and pale to nearly white.

ANGEL FACE (floribunda; 1968)

Lavender. Rose and red tints enliven the deep lavender of ruffled, very full, very fragrant blossoms, borne in clusters on a low, spreading, heavy-blooming plant. Bronze-tinted deep green leaves complete the picture. For the climbing sport, see page 77. AARS 1969.

TOP LEFT: Abraham Darby   TOP RIGHT: Alba Meidiland
MIDDLE LEFT: All That Jazz   MIDDLE RIGHT: Amber Queen
BOTTOM LEFT: Angel Face   BOTTOM RIGHT: Belle Story

BALLERINA (hybrid musk; 1937)

Pink and white. Single, white-centered pink flowers with the airy charm of dogwood or apple blossoms are carried in large, domed clusters. Tiny red hips will form if you don't remove the spent flowers. Glossy, elongated leaflets densely clothe a rounded shrub to about 5 feet tall.

BELLE STORY (English rose; 1984)

Peach pink. Shell-like petals unfold around a central tuft of stamens to give each large semi-double bloom the look of a warm pink peony. Borne in small clusters, the softly charming blossoms have an unusual fragrance: some say anise, others myrrh. The vigorous, 4-foot plant has dark green, fairly disease-resistant foliage; it blooms continuously throughout the growing season.

BETTY PRIOR (floribunda; 1935)

Deep pink. Here is all the charm of a wild rose and much of the vigor as well. Red buds open to single carmine pink blossoms that resemble dogwood blooms in size and shape. The plant is free blooming and strong growing, a tough, cold-tolerant shrub to about 6 feet high and wide.

BLANC DOUBLE DE COUBERT (hybrid rugosa; 1892)

White. Pointed buds surrounded by elongated sepals flare open to highly fragrant, fairly full but loose blossoms of purest white; orange hips develop after the flowers fade. The vigorous plant reaches about 6 feet, with dark, leathery, rugose foliage that colors well in autumn.

BONICA (shrub; 1985)

Clear pink. Arching canes form a mounding, spreading shrub to about 5 feet high, decked out in plenty of dark, glossy leaves. Sparkling against this good-looking background are large clusters of symmetrical, 3-inch double flowers in cake-frosting pink. Bright orange hips provide autumn decoration. AARS 1987.

BRASS BAND (floribunda; 1993)

Yellow and orange. Not loud, as the name would suggest, but certainly warm and bright. The plump, ovoid buds are yellow (since they show only the petal backs), but they open to full, shapely flowers displaying a medley of coppery apricot tones on the petal surfaces. The glossy-leafed bush reaches about 3 feet high. AARS 1995.

TOP: Ballerina
MIDDLE LEFT: Betty Prior   MIDDLE RIGHT: Blanc Double de Coubert
BOTTOM LEFT: Bonica   BOTTOM RIGHT: Brass Band

TOP: Buff Beauty
BOTTOM LEFT: Carefree Beauty   BOTTOM RIGHT: Carefree Wonder

BREDON (English rose; 1984)

Cream and peach blend. Small, petal-packed, pleasantly fragrant rosettes are borne in many-flowered sprays on an upright, floribunda-style bush to about 4 feet. The plump buds are cream colored, opening to creamy buff blossoms that deepen to golden peach or apricot in the centers.

BUFF BEAUTY (hybrid musk; 1939)

Golden apricot. Small clusters of 2- to 3-inch, very full, shapely flowers open a glowing golden apricot, then fade to creamy buff. Leaflets are broad and deeply veined; new foliage is a plum-bronze color. The arching, 6- to 8-foot shrub can easily be trained as a small climber.

CAREFREE BEAUTY (shrub; 1977)

Rose pink. An upright, spreading bush to 6 feet tall, 'Carefree Beauty' resembles a floribunda in plant habit and flower style. Long buds in small clusters open into semidouble, rich pink flowers; orange hips form in autumn and can last through winter. The foliage is good looking and disease resistant. This is one of the hardy Buck hybrids, developed to survive Iowa winters unprotected.

CAREFREE DELIGHT (shrub; 1993)

Light pink and white. Like 'Carefree Beauty', this one has disease resistance, overall vigor, and enhanced hardiness. The mounding-spreading plant is densely foliaged in small, dark leaves and reaches about 5 feet high; from spring to autumn, it's covered in a froth of clustered single, soft pink blossoms with distinct white centers. AARS 1996.

CAREFREE WONDER (shrub; 1990)

Pink and white. There's a lively look to these flowers: the clustered 3-inch, semidouble, carmine pink blossoms are backed in creamy white, with a bit of white infusing the petal margins as well. Upright (to about 5 feet) and bushy, the plant has the same easy-care qualities as the two varieties just described. It makes a good hedge. AARS 1991.

CÉCILE BRUNNER (polyantha; 1881)

Soft pink. Perfect miniature replicas of hybrid tea flowers bloom in graceful, thin-stemmed clusters. If left largely to its own devices, the bush will grow in time to a rounded 4 to 5 feet. A larger, fountainlike shrub form is 'Spray Cécile Brunner'. For the climbing sport, see page 77.

CHAMPLAIN (shrub; 1982)

Red. Informally double, dark red, 2½-inch blossoms come in floribundalike clusters on a bushy, 3- to 4-foot plant with dark, glossy leaves. One of the Canadian Explorer series, able to survive southern Canadian winters unprotected.

TOP LEFT: Cécile Brunner   TOP RIGHT: Champlain
MIDDLE LEFT: Charisma   MIDDLE RIGHT: Complicata
BOTTOM LEFT: Cornelia   BOTTOM RIGHT: Delicata

CHARISMA (floribunda; 1977)

Yellow and red blend. A rounded, spreading bush to 3 feet high flaunts small, very full rosettes of brilliant golden yellow with orange-red edges. As the flowers age, the petals become entirely suffused with red. Foliage is dark and glossy. AARS 1978.

CHERRY MEIDILAND (shrub; 1994)

Red and white. A 4- to 6-foot mound of color from spring to frost, this glossy-leafed shrub bears ruffled single blossoms in lively cherry red with conspicuous white centers. Orange hips continue the color show through autumn and winter.

CHINA DOLL (polyantha; 1946)

Rose pink. Rounded clusters of very full, 1- to 2-inch flowers may appear in such abundance that the glossy bright green leaves are almost obscured. The plant is low growing (reaching just 1½ feet tall) and nearly thornless.

COMPLICATA (species hybrid; date unknown)

Rose pink. It flowers only in spring—but its bloom is a genuine event. The large single flowers are brilliant pink, their golden stamens nestled in a circle of white petal bases. The arching canes, clothed in gracefully tapered leaves, form a broad, mounded shrub 5 to 6 feet tall; the plant can also be trained as a small climber.

CORNELIA (hybrid musk; 1925)

Pink blend. Elongated clusters of small, rosette-shaped flowers exhibit an intriguing range of colors: they open coral salmon, fade to peach, and finish a creamy buff pink with an elusive lavender cast. The arching canes are covered in glossy leaves with elongated leaflets. Leave the plant untrained to form a mounded shrub to about 6 feet, or train it as a small climber.

DELICATA (hybrid rugosa; 1898)

Lilac pink. The cool pink of the scented, semidouble, silky-petaled blossoms contrasts well with the dark, dense rugosa foliage. After the flowers fade, you'll get a good crop of bright orange hips. The bush reaches about 3 feet high.

EMPRESS JOSEPHINE (hybrid gallica; date unknown)

Rose pink. Judging from the blossoms, you'd suspect this spring-blooming hybrid was a tree peony masquerading as a rose. Very full flowers are composed of cool rose pink petals, lightly veined and shaded in darker pink. The compact, bushy plant reaches about 3 feet, its nearly thornless canes outfitted in grayish green, corrugated leaves. The name commemorates Napoleon's empress, who established the famed rose garden at Château Malmaison.

ENGLISH GARDEN (English rose; 1986)

Apricot and yellow blend. The flower form is consistent—flat, 3½-inch-wide blossoms packed with swirled petals—but the color is delightfully capricious. Sometimes it's more of a gold-shaded apricot, paling to buff cream at the petal edges; in warm weather, it can be a glowing orange yellow, with the softer apricot shades almost entirely absent. The upright, bushy plant reaches a height of about 4 feet; the leaves are light green.

TOP LEFT: Felicia TOP RIGHT: Flower Carpet
MIDDLE LEFT: Frau Dagmar Hartopp MIDDLE RIGHT: French Lace
BOTTOM LEFT: Gene Boerner BOTTOM RIGHT: Gertrude Jekyll

ERFURT (hybrid musk; 1939)

Pink and cream. Creamy ivory petals broadly edged in dark rose pink give the large, slightly more than single blossoms a luminous, lit-from-within appearance. Arching canes clothed in bronze-tinted foliage form a 6-foot, mounding plant.

EUROPEANA (floribunda; 1963)

Rich red. The spreading, strong-growing bush reaches 2½ to 3 feet tall, producing great clusters of full, 3-inch rosettes in an unfading, deep but bright red. Disease-resistant, bronze-tinted foliage completes the picture. AARS 1968.

FAIR BIANCA (English rose; 1982)

White. Its floral perfection frequently elicits comparisons to the damask 'Mme. Hardy' (page 23): the ivory to white blossoms are flat and circular, their petals packed around a green central eye, their myrrh fragrance a delight to the nose. The prickly-stemmed, dark-foliaged plant grows upright to about 3 feet.

FELICIA (hybrid musk; 1928)

Soft pink. The blooms are on the border between floribunda and hybrid tea: shapely, clustered buds open to fragrant, semidouble, ivory-infused pink flowers that age to blush pink. The bushy plant is about 6 feet high, with greater spread.

FIRST LIGHT (shrub; 1998)

Rose pink. The parents are 'Ballerina' and 'Bonica', so it's no wonder the child is outstanding. Carried in large clusters, the nearly circular single flowers are a clear rose pink with contrasting dark red stamens. The dense, rounded, glossy-leafed bush is smaller than either parent, to about 3 feet high and wide. AARS 1998.

F. J. GROOTENDORST (hybrid rugosa; 1918)

Cherry red. The small, fully double flowers have fringed petal margins that give them the look of carnations. Clusters of these unusual blossoms come on a robust, healthy bush outfitted in rugosa-style foliage; the plant grows about 5 feet high, with greater spread. There are several color sports, including 'Pink Grootendorst' (page 67) and 'White Grootendorst'.

FLOWER CARPET (ground cover; 1989)

Dark pink. Low (to about 2 feet tall) and spreading, this rose is suited to mass planting as a ground cover, but it also serves nicely as a border planting or individual shrub. Clusters of semidouble, carmine pink flowers bloom against a background of dense, glossy, disease-resistant foliage. 'White Flower Carpet' is identical in habit and foliage, but its flowers are white.

FLUTTERBYE (shrub; 1996)

Yellow and pink blend. The ruffled single flowers are attractive in form, and their mutable color is an added charm. Pointed, red-tinged yellow buds open to yellow flowers that change to creamy buff, pink, and coral; all these colors are often present in the flowers within a single cluster. Ultra-glossy foliage clothes a husky plant that makes a fountain-like 6- to 10-foot shrub or small climber in mild climates, a more compact (but still large) shrub where winters are colder.

FRAU DAGMAR HARTOPP (Fru Dagmar Hastrup) (hybrid rugosa; 1914)

Soft pink. Fragrant, silvery pink single flowers and showy red hips adorn a compact, 4- to 6-foot plant with typical rugosa foliage. Grown on its own roots, it can form sizable clumps.

FRENCH LACE (floribunda; 1980)

Creamy white. Buff-shaded ivory buds in small clusters swirl open to creamy, full-petaled blossoms with apricot centers. The bushy plant reaches about 4 feet and has dark, glossy foliage; it's not as cold hardy as most other floribundas. AARS 1982.

GARTENDIREKTOR OTTO LINNE (shrub; 1934)

Dark pink. An ancestry combining wichuraiana rambler, hybrid musk, and polyantha produced this virtuous shrub, whose only flaw may be its rather long name! Large, tapered clusters of small but very full blossoms appear on an upright to fountainlike plant around 5 feet tall. The apple green leaves have narrow, elongated leaflets.

GENE BOERNER (floribunda; 1968)

Rose pink. In every detail, the buds and full blossoms are small-scale replicas of the best hybrid teas. Lightly fragrant flowers in an even shade of rosy pink come both singly and in clusters, on an upright plant to about 4 feet. AARS 1969.

GERTRUDE JEKYLL (English rose; 1986)

Bright pink. One parent, the Portland 'Comte de Chambord' (page 32), strongly influenced this variety's floral style: petal-crammed flowers in bright, warm pink open flat from fat buds that appear in clusters at the ends of very thorny stems. Vigor is a strong point. In mild climates, this rose produces long canes (to 10 feet) and is best trained as a climber; in colder regions, it's a large, arching shrub. In any climate, its strong damask fragrance is notable.

GINGERSNAP (floribunda; 1978)

Orange. Ruffled, glowing orange petals are packed into very full flowers of nearly hybrid tea size. Clusters of these vivid blooms appear on a rounded, bushy plant to about 3 feet tall; the foliage is a deep bronze purple when new, maturing to dark green.

GRAHAM THOMAS (English rose; 1983)

Yellow. Plump, red-tinted yellow buds open to 3½-inch, cupped blossoms filled with petals of the brightest butter yellow. Modest clusters of the glowing blooms are carried at the ends of arching canes that reach 10 feet or more in length. The vigorous plant can be grown as a climber in mild-winter climates; where winter weather is colder, it's a slender, tall shrub.

Graham Thomas

GYPSY DANCER (shrub; 1995)

Orange, red, and yellow blend. As you might expect from the name, these are lively flowers: semidouble blooms with wavy-edged yellow-orange petals heavily brushed in red. Clusters of these 3-inch fireballs glow against a backdrop of dark foliage on a spreading, 4-foot-tall bush.

HANSA (hybrid rugosa; 1905)

Purple red. This rose has all the good qualities for which the rugosas are noted. The bushy plant, covered with handsome rugose foliage, reaches about 6 feet high and wide and makes a superlative hedge. The richly colored, clove-scented double flowers are plentiful in spring and fall, with scattered bloom through summer; orange-red hips provide flashy autumn decoration.

HERITAGE (English rose; 1984)

Soft pink. The outer petals form a cupped circle that cradles the bloom center—a crowd of folded, swirled, shell pink petals faintly infused with apricot. Small clusters of these fragrant medium-size flowers come on a sparsely thorned, vigorous plant that reaches a bushy 5 feet.

ICEBERG (floribunda; 1958)

White. This bushy, vigorous plant is not your typical floribunda. It's taller (to 6 feet), with small clusters of long, pointed buds that open to sweet-scented blooms of nearly hybrid tea size. The dense, glossy foliage is a medium to dark green. For the climbing sport, see page 77.

Iceberg

IMPATIENT (floribunda; 1982)

Orange red. Is it red or is it orange? Vivid orange-scarlet buds, freely produced on upright plants growing 3 to 3½ feet high, open to 3-inch blossoms of a softer shade. Mahogany-hued new growth, a good complement to the flower color, matures to glossy dark green. AARS 1984.

INTRIGUE (floribunda; 1982)

Purple red. In overall appearance, this floridunda may as well be a small hybrid tea. Globular, black-purple buds open to ruffled, moderately full, plum-colored blossoms with a strong citrusy scent. The plant is rounded, bushy, and dark foliaged; it reaches about 3 feet high. AARS 1984.

Intrigue

TOP: Heritage
BOTTOM LEFT: Hansa   BOTTOM RIGHT: Heritage

GRÜSS AN AACHEN (floribunda; 1909)

Pink and cream. Although it's traditionally grouped with the floribundas, this exquisite rose bears no relation to the other members of the class: while they derive from polyanthas and hybrid teas, 'Grüss an Aachen' has a different ancestry and might be regarded as the last of the shrubby Bourbons or as a forebear of contemporary English roses. Small clusters of fat buds open to flat, full, creamy pink to ivory flowers rather like smaller versions of 'Souvenir de la Malmaison' (page 33). The plant is compact and bushy, reaching about 3 feet tall. 'Pink Grüss an Aachen' is a darker color sport.

KATHLEEN (hybrid musk; 1922)

Pale pink. Reminiscent of apple blossoms, the blush pink single flowers—each about the size of a half dollar—appear in airy clusters that become sprays of bright hips in autumn. Gray-green leaves with elongated leaflets clothe a vigorous, arching bush to about 6 feet; it can be trained as a small climber.

LAVENDER LASSIE (hybrid musk; 1960)

Lilac pink. Bouquetlike clusters of ruffled double blooms in a shade somewhere between lavender and pink strike a cool note in the garden. Glossy, disease-resistant leaves cover a robust plant that can be maintained as a large (6- to 8-foot) shrub but is more often trained as a modest climber.

L. D. BRAITHWAITE (English rose; 1988)

Crimson. The rich flower color comes from its parent 'The Squire'; blossom shape and plant quality derive from the other parent, 'Mary Rose'. The 4-inch blossoms open wide and cupped with outer petals reflexed; they retain their red color without bluing. Prickly canes and stems form an upright to slightly spreading bush about 5 feet high.

LINDA CAMPBELL (hybrid rugosa; 1990)

Bright red. The foliage is less textured than that of most rugosa hybrids, and the velvety, moderately double blossoms are the purest red, lacking the typical rugosa purple tinge. Large clusters of blooms come on an arching plant to 8 feet tall.

LIVIN' EASY (floribunda; 1992)

Orange apricot. Plentiful high-gloss foliage would make this an attractive shrub even if it didn't bloom. Add the glowing, moderately double blossoms, though, and you have a garden beacon throughout the growing season. The rounded bush reaches about 3 feet; it's good for foreground planting and border hedges. AARS 1996.

MAGIC CARPET (ground cover; 1992)

Lilac pink. The magic is in the profusion of flowers: sizable clusters of small, semidouble, cool lilac pink blossoms that come ceaselessly throughout the growing season, adorning a spreading, low plant (to just 1½ feet tall) bearing small, glossy leaves.

MARGARET MERRILL (floribunda; 1978)

White. A child of the superlative white hybrid tea 'Pascali' (page 49), with the same admirable form. Small clusters of pointed, off-white buds open to pure white, semidouble blooms with ruffled petals and a strong perfume blending citrus and spice. The bushy plant grows to 5 feet tall and features leathery dark green foliage.

TOP: Iceberg
MIDDLE: Lavender Lassie
BOTTOM LEFT: L.D. Braithwaite BOTTOM RIGHT: Margaret Merrill

MARGO KOSTER (polyantha; 1931)

Light orange. Nearly round buds composed of many shell-like petals unfurl to small, cupped, light orange flowers resembling ranunculus blossoms. The blooms come in large clusters on a twiggy, 1½- to 2-foot-tall plant bearing glossy light green foliage. This is the best-known member of a large family of color sports, including rose pink 'Dick Koster', rosy red 'Mothersday', orange-red 'Orange Mothersday', and 'Snow White'.

MARTIN FROBISHER (hybrid rugosa; 1968)

Pink and white. Very double but informal flowers are pastel confections of soft pink shaded white, carried in small clusters on a dense, rounded bush that reaches about 6 feet high and wide. The gray-green foliage reveals little of the plant's rugosa ancestry, though it does have the typical rugosa disease resistance. This is one of the Canadian Explorer roses, bred to survive southern Canadian winters unprotected.

MARY ROSE (English rose; 1983)

Dark pink. Rather like a truly perpetual hybrid perpetual, 'Mary Rose' delivers fully double, broadly cup-shaped, lightly fragrant pink blossoms with outer petals that reflex to form a circular frame. The free-flowering, bushy plant grows 4 to 6 feet high and wide, its prickly stems clothed in dark green foliage.

Mary Rose

MME. PLANTIER (hybrid alba; 1835)

White. This tall, arching plant blooms in spring, bearing exquisite 2-inch blossoms that capture the essence of old rose beauty. Plump, red-tinted ivory buds open to flat, circular blossoms packed with folded petals; the blooms often show a green central eye. Grown as a shrub, 'Mme. Plantier' can reach 8 feet tall, but it also can be trained as a small climber or encouraged to clamber into trees, where its slender, nearly thornless canes will spill gracefully from the branches. The foliage is a soft green.

MORDEN BLUSH (shrub; 1988)

Light pink. The pastel charm of its blooms belies this plant's toughness and cold hardiness—it can endure northern winters without protection. Clusters of medium-size, soft pink buds swirl open to fully double, fairly flat flowers that fade to ivory. The bushy plant grows upright to about 4 feet, clothed in plenty of dark green foliage.

TOP: Margo Koster
MIDDLE LEFT: Margo Koster   MIDDLE RIGHT: Mme. Plantier
BOTTOM: Mary Rose (foreground) and Perdita

NEARLY WILD (floribunda; 1941)

Deep pink and white. The name refers to the flowers: clusters of single, white-centered pink blooms with the simple charm of wild roses. The plant is dense and mounding, reaching about 4 feet tall. The plentiful foliage is susceptible to black spot in warm, humid regions.

NEVADA (shrub; 1927)

White. Early in spring, the long, arching canes carry 4-inch, nearly single, pink-tinted white blossoms all along their length; bloom is less profuse over summer, but there's another satisfying burst in autumn. The spreading bush reaches about 8 feet, with dark stems and soft gray-green leaves. 'Marguerite Hilling' is a pink-flowered sport.

OTHELLO (English rose; 1986)

Crimson. Globular buds open to 4- to 5-inch, cupped to flat, powerfully fragrant blossoms packed with countless petals; the red color is brighter in warm conditions, darker and more sultry in cool weather, and takes on an increasingly purple cast as the flowers age. The plant is in proportion to the large blossoms: it's tall (to 8 feet) and robust, often seen trained as a restrained climber.

PENELOPE (hybrid musk; 1924)

Warm pink blend. Coral orange buds in medium-size clusters open to fluffy semidouble blossoms that vary from creamy pink or apricot to buff cream, according to weather and season. Autumn brings a subtly showy display of coral pink hips. Dense, shrubby growth to about 6 feet makes this one a good choice for hedges.

PERDITA (English rose; 1983)

Apricot, gold, and cream blend. Borne in small clusters, the 3-inch, cupped blossoms open flat, crowded with folded and swirled petals. The color varies: the blooms may be golden apricot fading to creamy peach, or they may be a more intense golden amber that gradually changes to buff cream. Bronzed canes with dark green leaves form a bushy plant about 4 feet high and wide.

PERLE D'OR (polyantha; 1884)

Orange blend. Like 'Cécile Brunner', this one has small hybrid tea–style buds, but they are orange apricot rather than pink. The open blossoms are filled with numerous narrow petals; depending on the weather, they vary from golden orange to apricot to yellowish peach as they unfurl, but always fade to pinkish buff with age. Flowers come singly or in clusters on a plant that, in mild regions, can reach 6 feet high with greater spread. The foliage is plum bronze when new, maturing to dark green.

TOP LEFT: Nevada   TOP RIGHT: Pink Grootendorst
BOTTOM LEFT: Penelope   BOTTOM RIGHT: Playboy

PINK GROOTENDORST (hybrid rugosa; 1923)

Rose pink. Fringed petal margins give the small, double, deep pink blossoms the look of carnations. Plentiful clusters of blooms come on a vigorous, spreading, prickly bush that can attain 6 feet or more; the foliage is somewhat rugose.

PINK MEIDILAND (shrub; 1985)

Deep pink and white. Compared to the other Meidiland roses (the alba, cherry, scarlet, and white members of the group are described in this chapter), 'Pink Meidiland' is a bushy plant rather than a mounding-spreading to trailing one. Upright-growing, well-foliaged plants to about 4 feet are adorned with clusters of 2½-inch, deep pink single flowers made especially showy by their conspicuous white centers.

PLAYBOY (floribunda; 1976)

Orange, red, and yellow blend. Clustered, single, 3½-inch blossoms bring fiery color in the garden. The flowers' yellow centers blend out to orange; the petals are brushed and infused with red toward the margins. The compact, glossy-leafed shrub reaches about 3 feet high.

TOP LEFT: Queen Nefertiti   TOP RIGHT: Raubritter
BOTTOM LEFT: Sally Holmes   BOTTOM RIGHT: Scarlet Meidiland

QUEEN NEFERTITI (English rose; 1988)

Pink and yellow blend. Thanks to the highly changeable flower color, catalog descriptions (and photographs) of this rose vary widely. The full, cupped to flat flowers—often revealing a button eye when open—start as a yellowish apricot, then finish with a pinker look. The plant is bushy, upright, and compact, growing about 4 feet high.

RAUBRITTER (shrub; 1936)

Rose pink. This spring-blooming rose is instantly identifiable by its near-hemispherical blooms and relaxed habit. There is no other rose like it. Opening from globular buds, the cupped, 2½-inch flowers with shell-like petals blanket a mounding, spreading plant that's lax enough to trail over walls or down a slope. It grows to about 3 feet tall and twice as wide; the leaves are grayish green.

RED RIBBONS (ground cover; 1990)

Bright red. Bright yellow stamens center semidouble, lipstick red flowers that come in clusters on a low (to 2-foot-tall), spreading plant with plenty of dark green foliage.

REGENSBURG (floribunda; 1979)

Pink and white. Pretty but unassuming, the pinkish ivory buds give no hint of the striking blooms to come: moderately full, strawberry pink flowers with white centers, brushings of white on the petal edges, and nearly white petal backs. Crisp, glossy foliage covers a rounded plant growing just 2 feet tall.

ROSERAIE DE L'HAŸ
(hybrid rugosa; 1901)

Crimson. Tapered buds unfold into blowsy, deep red, pleasantly spicy-scented blossoms that become increasingly purple with age. The shrub is large (to 6 feet tall and wide), thorny, and densely clothed in apple green leaves; unlike most rugosa derivatives, it doesn't set many hips.

Roseraie de l'Haÿ

ROYAL BONICA (shrub; 1994)

Rose pink. It's hard to improve on 'Bonica', but this "royal" edition does give you flowers that are more double and a bit larger, in a deeper pink. The plant, though, is the same: a rounded shrub to about 5 feet high, covered in disease-resistant, dark green foliage.

SALLY HOLMES (shrub; 1976)

Pinkish ivory. Single, pink-blushed white flowers—like 3-inch apple blossoms—appear in large to truly huge clusters. Outstanding as a rounded, glossy-leafed, large shrub (to 8 feet tall), the plant can also be trained as a climber.

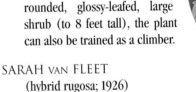

Sally Holmes

SARAH VAN FLEET
(hybrid rugosa; 1926)

Rose pink. The hybrid tea half of its parentage shows in the form of the buds and the semidouble, silken-petaled, somewhat fruity-scented blossoms. The plant is tall (reaching about 8 feet), with light green leaves. 'Mary Manners' is a white-flowered sport.

SCARLET MEIDILAND (shrub; 1987)

Bright red. Small, fully double, ruffled blossoms in unfading scarlet come in great clusters that can weigh down the branches. The husky, glossy-leafed shrub makes an arching mound to about 4 feet high and 6 feet across; it's a good choice for barrier and informal hedge plantings.

SCENTIMENTAL (floribunda; 1996)

 Red and white. Instantly recognizable, the variably striped and marbled blossoms combine rich red and chalk white. Flower shape—from the plump buds to the open flowers—is attractive as well, and the fragrance is, of course, notable. Textured dark green leaves cover a rounded bush to about 3½ feet high. AARS 1997.

SEA FOAM (shrub; 1964)

 White. A creamy foam of clustered, full, rosette-shaped blossoms billows on a sea of dark, glossy leaves. The spreading plant reaches about 3 feet high and twice as wide; the main canes are lax and trailing.

SEVILLANA (floribunda; 1982)

 Scarlet. This one has the typical floribunda stiffness, though it's larger (to about 5 feet) and bulkier than the usual. Clusters of almost double, fire-bright blossoms nearly cover the upright, bushy plant; the leaves are dark red when new, maturing to deep green.

SHOWBIZ (floribunda; 1981)

Scarlet. Rounded, compact, and short (just 2 feet tall), this one furnishes great trusses of intense, orange-tinted scarlet blossoms that look like brilliant pompons against the glossy, dark foliage. It's excellent as a border hedge or container plant. AARS 1985.

SIMPLICITY (floribunda; 1978)

Rose pink. Classed as a floribunda but promoted as a shrub, this bushy 3- to 4-foot plant is easily maintained as an everblooming hedge. Slender, pointed buds in small clusters open to semidouble, cupped, bright rose pink blossoms. 'Red Simplicity' and 'White Simplicity' are in the same mold as the original pink version, but they are not color sports of it.

SINGIN' IN THE RAIN (floribunda; 1991)

Apricot blend. The changeable color is hard to nail down: the blooms have been called golden apricot or russet orange, often with a brownish cast described in catalogs as "cinnamon." Small clusters of urn-shaped buds unfold to 3½-inch, sweet-scented double blossoms. The bushy, upright plant reaches about 5 feet and features glossy, dark foliage. AARS 1995.

SIR THOMAS LIPTON (hybrid rugosa; 1900)

 Creamy white. Bushy and bulky (to 8 feet high and wide), this one has plenty of leathery dark green foliage to serve as a backdrop for the well-shaped, scented, semidouble blossoms it bears both individually and in small clusters.

SNOW OWL (White Pavement) (hybrid rugosa; 1989)

White. Just 3 to 4 feet tall, this stocky, bushy plant is small for a hybrid rugosa, though its medium green foliage is of the typical rugosa type. Slender white buds open to semidouble, cupped blossoms centered with showy bright yellow stamens.

TOP LEFT: Scentimental   TOP RIGHT: Sevillana
MIDDLE: Sea Foam
BOTTOM LEFT: Showbiz   BOTTOM RIGHT: Simplicity

SPARRIESHOOP (shrub; 1953)

Pink. Like clusters of bright butterflies, the ruffled, 4-inch single flowers rest against the leaves. The big, voluptuous shrub easily reaches 8 feet tall; it has bronzy new growth and bronze-tinted mature foliage. 'Weisse aus Sparrieshoop' ('White Sparrieshoop') is a sport with white flowers that are infused with pink in cool weather.

STANWELL PERPETUAL (hybrid spinosissima; 1838)

Pale pink. Full, damask-type, blush pink blossoms appear from spring into autumn on a twiggy plant with small gray-green leaves. The canes arch over to make a rounded bush 4 to 6 feet high.

SUMMER FASHION (floribunda; 1986)

Pink and yellow. Here are confectionlike blossoms in a delicious combination of soft, warm colors. The short, ovoid buds are cream and yellow with a pink edge on the outer petals; as the very full, fragrant blossoms age, more pink infuses the petals. The plant is bushy and compact, reaching just 2½ feet tall.

SUN FLARE (floribunda; 1981)

Lemon yellow. Compact, bushy plants to about 2½ feet high produce great quantities of shapely, fragrant, 3-inch blossoms in clusters of small to moderate size. The luminous, nearly unfading lemon color is beautifully displayed against the bright green, extra-glossy foliage. The climbing sport is sold as 'Yellow Blaze'. AARS 1983.

SUNSPRITE (floribunda; 1977)

Bright yellow. Small clusters of ovoid buds open to fragrant, wavy-petaled, brilliant yellow blossoms that retain their color until petals fall. The free-flowering, upright bush, clothed in semiglossy leaves, reaches about 3 feet tall.

TAMORA (English rose; 1983)

Orange blend. Plump, nearly red buds unfurl to full, cupped to flat, highly fragrant blossoms that offer a veritable fruit salad of color: gold-shaded apricot, peach, and orange, grading and fading to creamy buff. The blooms come profusely on an upright, prickly, fairly short bush (to about 3 feet tall) with dark green leaves.

Tamora

TOP LEFT: Sparrieshoop TOP RIGHT: Sun Flare
MIDDLE LEFT: Stanwell Perpetual MIDDLE RIGHT: Sunsprite
BOTTOM: The Fairy

THE FAIRY (polyantha; 1932)

🌺 Light pink. The small, full-petaled flowers have no special individual beauty; their garden value lies in their great profusion. From spring straight through into autumn, they bloom in elongated, pyramidal clusters, covering the spreading, about 3-foot-tall bush in a pale pink cloak. The leaves are small, glossy, and diseaseproof.

THÉRÈSE BUGNET (hybrid rugosa; 1950)

🌺 Lilac pink. Slender, nearly red buds open to double, cool lilac pink flowers with a fluffy, informal quality. The plant grows upright to about 6 feet, with reddish stems and bluish green foliage composed of narrow, slightly rugose leaflets that turn red with chilly autumn weather. This rose is extremely cold tolerant, taking Canadian and prairie winters without protection.

THE SQUIRE (English rose; 1977)

🌺 Dark red. For heady perfume, this rose is second to none. And the blossoms are as memorable as the scent: large, velvety, and black tinged, with a petal complexity like that of the Bourbon 'Souvenir de la Malmaison' (page 33). In its height (to about 4 feet) and stiff, upright habit—and in its susceptibility to mildew—the plant could pass for an old red hybrid tea.

The Squire

THE WIFE OF BATH (English rose; 1969)

🌺 Rose pink. One of the first English roses to be developed, 'The Wife of Bath' is still a worthy choice. It blooms profusely, bearing cupped, peonylike flowers composed of shell-like petals; the blossom centers are deeper pink and show clusters of yellow stamens. The bushy, upright plant reaches about 4 feet, with plum-bronze new growth that matures to dark green.

TOPAZ JEWEL (hybrid rugosa; 1988)

🌺 Yellow. The unusual marriage of a yellow miniature and a pink hybrid rugosa produced this arching, 6-foot-tall shrub. Its attractive buds and double, 3½-inch, butter yellow blossoms come in small clusters; the dark foliage shows some of the classic rugosa texture.

TRUMPETER (floribunda; 1977)

🌺 Orange red. Intense, blazing color—somewhere between orange and red—is displayed in very full, ruffled blossoms

The Wife of Bath

that are somewhat larger than those of the average floribunda. Carried individually and in clusters, the blossoms appear on a compact, bushy, 2- to 2½-foot plant with glossy foliage—a good choice for a foreground accent or border hedge.

WATERMELON ICE (ground cover; 1996)

🌺 Deep pink. Semidouble blossoms in showy watermelon pink with paler centers come in many-flowered clusters on a glossy-leafed, mounding-spreading plant that reaches just 1½ feet high.

WENLOCK (English rose; 1984)

🌺 Crimson. Full-petaled, cupped to flat, headily perfumed flowers of rich red take on purple tints as they expand. Vigor is a strong point: the bushy plant easily reaches 5 feet in climates with a definite winter, and in warm-winter areas, it's larger still and grows readily as a climber.

WHITE MEIDILAND (shrub; 1987)

🌺 White. This one resembles its stablemate 'Alba Meidiland' in habit, flower form, and flower color—but its clustered, very double white blossoms are twice as large, and the plant is lower growing and more spreading, to about 2 feet high and 6 feet wide.

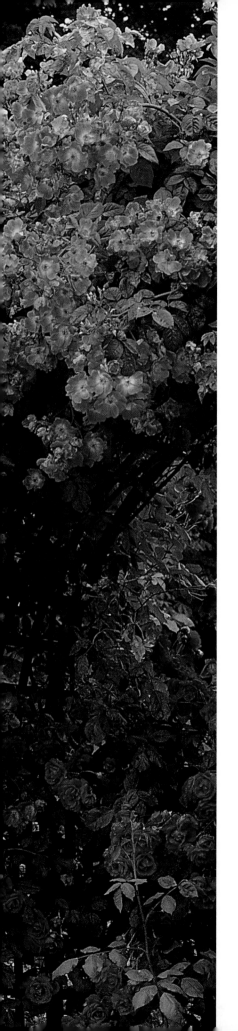

When you choose climbing roses, you can plan garden decoration: blossoms to cover a wall, festoon a fence, prettify a pergola, or even trail from the branches of a tree. There's a wealth of varieties at your disposal—restrained climbers and more rampant ones, spring-flowering types and repeat bloomers, with blossoms that range from small to large and come in every rose color imaginable.

CLIMBING
ROSES

Because all climbers need several years to establish before they produce enough growth to create the desired effect, it's especially important to choose your varieties carefully. Removing a poor selection and starting all over again wastes a significant amount of time. Obviously, it pays to make an informed decision; keep in mind that climbers vary in size, in vigor of growth, and in hardiness. Check each one's characteristics before you buy.

Another point to remember is that climbing roses are not climbers in the sense of clematis, ivy, honeysuckle, or wisteria. They have no actual means of attaching themselves to a support; thorns only help long canes scramble through trees or shrubs. You'll need to train and tie any climber in its early years if it is to go where you want it to go. That said, the need for subsequent training will vary somewhat depending on the particular rose and on where you plant it. Sorts that produce

For romantic atmosphere, nothing surpasses an arbor lushly blanketed in the scented blossoms of a climbing rose.

many new canes (or, at least, much new growth) each year require annual training to remain neat and tidy. Climbers used on walls, fences, and arbors also need at least yearly training and pruning to keep them within their prescribed spaces, while those growing on pergolas or climbing into trees can get by with much more casual attention once they've filled the desired space.

To help guide your choices, the climbers described in this chapter are identified according to type or class (see below). Most retail nurseries do not stock a great variety; climbing roses don't sell as well as bush kinds, since their garden use is limited (how many can an average garden hold?). Look to mail-order suppliers for the widest selection.

CLIMBING SPORTS. Many bush roses have produced climbing sports, identical to the bush form except for their long, more or less pliable climbing canes. You'll find them in modern rose classes such as hybrid tea, grandiflora, and floribunda, as well as in a number of old rose types (China, Bourbon, and hybrid perpetual, for example). All are repeat flowering.

KORDESII CLIMBERS. Derived from an artificial species, *Rosa × kordesii* (a tetraploid offspring of *R. wichuraiana* and *R. rugosa*), these roses possess the vigor of those species; the rugosa ancestry also contributes disease resistance and added hardiness. All are repeat flowering.

LARGE-FLOWERED CLIMBERS (LCL). These plants are natural climbers with no bush counterparts. Flowers may be borne individually or in clusters, and are about the size of hybrid tea blossoms. Many of these are repeat flowering, though a few favorites are exclusively spring blooming.

PILLAR-CLIMBERS. Some of the descriptions note that the rose is a pillar-climber or can be trained as one. These roses are the just-barely climbers that tend to produce upright-growing (but not quite stiffly upright) canes that will flower when trained upright, as on a post or pillar.

RAMBLERS. This group of (mostly) spring-flowering roses is noted for massive floral displays and a profusion of new canes produced after bloom; the new growth bears the next year's flow-

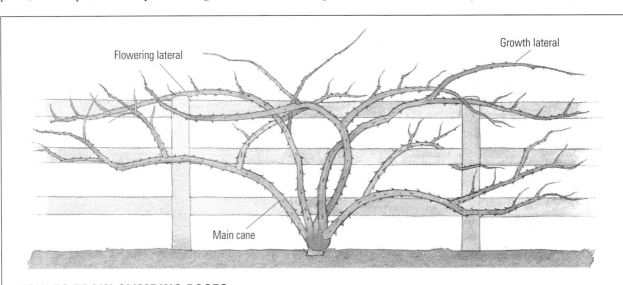

Growth lateral

Flowering lateral

Main cane

HOW TO TRAIN CLIMBING ROSES

Left to its own devices, a long climbing cane will attempt to grow upward. This is an example of apical dominance: the topmost growing point (apex) continues to grow at the expense of growth buds along its length that might produce lateral shoots. But when a long, upright cane is arched over or bent down to a horizontal position, the apex ceases to be dominant and many growth buds along the cane begin to grow, each one heading upward. Most will become flowering stems 8 to 16 inches long, but a few will maintain the climbing mode as growth laterals.

During its first year of growth, let a climbing cane grow upward, making no attempt at training. The next year, when it is mature, you can bend it from the vertical and tie it into place. If canes are fairly limber, you can angle them outward into hori-

zontal positions; if they're a bit stiffer, you may have to settle for spreading them into a vase outline. In either case, tie canes into place with their tips pointing downward, thus ending apical dominance. Follow the same procedure with growth laterals (which will then produce flowering laterals).

Some short, stiff-caned climbers (often called "pillar-climbers" or "pillar roses") will grow upright and still produce flowering laterals; these are more like narrow shrubs than actual climbers. You can train some of the limber-caned climbers ('New Dawn', for example) to decorate a post by spiraling the canes around the support, as shown on page 96. Trained in this manner, the canes depart far enough from the vertical to produce flowering laterals along their lengths.

ers. Ramblers are derived from several species. One common group is the wichuraiana ramblers, offspring of *Rosa wichuraiana;* they produce the most prolific new growth, particularly canes from ground level. Multiflora ramblers, offspring of *R. multiflora,* are equally vigorous but usually have fewer canes.

SPECIES HYBRIDS. This is a grab-bag category, cohesive because it includes roses immediately derived from a species. The descriptions identify the relevant species; 'Félicité et Perpétue', for example, is a hybrid sempervirens. With few exceptions, these flower only in spring.

The letters AARS at the end of an entry indicate that the rose has received the All-America Rose Selection Award (see page 123). For some roses, an alternate name is noted in parentheses. This may be the name by which the variety is known in other countries, or it may be an incorrect name under which it is sometimes marketed.

ALBERIC BARBIER (wichuraiana rambler; 1900)

Creamy white. Glossy dark green foliage is a backdrop for clusters of small yellow buds that open to creamy, yellow-centered blossoms absolutely packed with petals. In the cooler climates this rose prefers, it shows some scattered repeat bloom. The plant forms a framework of long-lasting main canes, from which much vigorous annual growth arises.

ALBERTINE (LCL; 1921)

Pink. A wichuraiana rambler by parentage—and like the wichuraiana ramblers, it flowers only in spring. The plant is less limber than most, though, and can even be grown as a giant, mounding shrub. Ovoid, nearly red buds open to silky, two-tone warm pink blossoms that bear some resemblance to small hybrid tea flowers.

ALCHYMIST (hybrid eglanteria; 1956)

Apricot blend. Clothed in glossy, bronzy green leaves, this restrained climber is versatile enough to be grown as a large shrub. The flower color is an indescribable, ever-changing melange of gold, yellow, apricot, and pink; the fully open blossoms have the flat, swirled and quartered form of some old garden roses.

ALISTER STELLA GRAY (Noisette; 1894). Yellow. See page 34.

ALOHA (LCL; 1949)

Pink. Its plentiful dark, glossy foliage and restrained growth habit make this a good choice for training upright as a pillar-climber or even growing as a free-standing large shrub. The large, full-petaled blossoms are rose pink with darker petal backs.

TOP LEFT: Alberic Barbier   TOP RIGHT: Alchymist   MIDDLE: Albertine   BOTTOM: Aloha

TOP TO BOTTOM: Altissimo, America, American Pillar

ALTISSIMO (LCL; 1966)

Red. Clusters of small buds open to spectacular single flowers of velvety bright red with central clusters of showy yellow stamens. Glossy leaves add to the brilliance. Train it as a small climber or pillar-climber, or maintain it as a tall shrub.

AMERICA (LCL; 1976)

Coral pink. This repeat bloomer has lovely, shapely buds and large, full, highly fragrant flowers of the best hybrid tea form. The vigorous plant has canes that reach about 15 feet; it can also be trained upright as a pillar-climber. AARS 1976.

AMERICAN PILLAR (wichuraiana rambler; 1902)

Deep pink. This extra-vigorous, glossy-leafed plant is a bit coarse, but it's tough enough to thrive without care and is hardy into southern New England. The lavish spring display features large clusters of single, silver dollar–size carmine pink blossoms with white centers.

ANEMONE (hybrid laevigata; 1896)

Pink. In spring, large single blossoms decorate the slightly gaunt plant like a flight of tropical butterflies. The rose pink blooms, with darker veining and paler petal backs, are complemented by gray-green foliage. 'Ramona' is a sport with rosy red flowers.

AWAKENING (LCL; 1935)

Pink. A sport of the famous 'New Dawn' and identical to it in growth, foliage, and flower color. The difference is in the fullness of the blossoms: each flower is packed with petals and opens flat, in the manner of many old European roses.

BELLE PORTUGAISE (hybrid gigantea; 1903)

Light pink. In mild-winter parts of the South, Southwest, and West, this rampant climber offers breathtaking displays in earliest spring. Especially long, tapered pink buds on long stems open to semidouble silvery pink blossoms. The plant produces a few massive main canes that bear leafy growth at some distance from the ground; use it to cover pergolas or roofs or to climb trees.

BLAZE (LCL; 1932)

Bright red. Every year, this rose blazes its way across the country. Clusters of scarlet, 2- to 3-inch double flowers cover the plant over a long spring bloom season, then continue in smaller bursts through summer and autumn. The plant is vigorous but not huge, ideal for fences, walls, and pillars. 'Blaze Improved' is reputed to be more reliably repeat flowering.

Blaze

BOBBIE JAMES (multiflora rambler; 1961)

White. A truly large (to 30 feet) and rambunctious climber, this one needs the support of a pergola, tree, or tall and open fence to display its springtime snow-mound of bloom to best advantage. Though the clusters of semidouble blossoms may be pendent, the buds and flowers face upward. Foliage is dense, with elegantly elongated leaflets.

TOP: Cl. Cécile Brunner
MIDDLE LEFT: Cl. Iceberg   MIDDLE RIGHT: Constance Spry
BOTTOM: Don Juan

CL. ANGEL FACE (floribunda; 1981)

Lavender. Everything that makes the bush form (see page 58) so popular is available in a climber that grows to about 10 feet.

CL. BLUE GIRL (Cl. Kölner Karnival) (hybrid tea; 1977)

Lavender. This climbing sport of the bush form (see page 42) is a modest grower to about 10 feet.

CL. CÉCILE BRUNNER (polyantha; 1894)

Pink. The exquisite buds of the bush form (see page 60) are available in a rampant climber that can reach 20 feet, forming a thicket of growth. The best strains flower repeatedly throughout the growing season; some strains flower primarily in spring, with just a scattering of later bloom.

CL. ÉTOILE DE HOLLANDE (hybrid tea; 1931)

Deep red. One of the most beloved of the red climbers, noted for its vigor (the plant reaches 15 feet or more) and full, intensely fragrant blossoms in rich, unfading red.

CL. FIRST PRIZE (hybrid tea; 1976)

Deep pink. A medium-size climber (to about 8 feet), with the same flawless buds and exhibition-quality flowers that made the bush form famous (see page 44).

CL. ICEBERG (floribunda; 1968)

White. Often rated the finest climbing white rose; some even call it the finest climber, period. Profuse flowering and good repeat bloom come on a vigorous plant that reaches 15 feet.

CL. LA FRANCE (hybrid tea; 1893)

Rose pink. A climbing sport of the first hybrid tea (see page 46), with the same full, fragrant, two-tone blossoms. The plant is a restrained climber to about 10 feet.

CL. PEACE (hybrid tea; 1950)

Yellow and pink blend. The full, ruffled blossoms made famous by the bush form (see page 49) come on a rampant, far-reaching climber that's entirely in proportion to the mammoth flowers. With canes that can reach 20 feet or more, the plant is best used on a fence or large wall.

CL. SOUVENIR DE LA MALMAISON (Bourbon; 1893)

Light pink. The bush form (see page 33) is of moderate size and slow to build up, but the climber is bursting with vigor. Canes grow to 15 feet or more (especially in mild climates), bearing a good spring crop of full-petaled flowers; repeat bloom is spotty and less profuse.

CONSTANCE SPRY (shrub/LCL; 1961)

Rich pink. A hybrid of the gallica 'Belle Isis' (see page 21), this one bears large, full, cupped blossoms in the style of the old European roses—and like them, it flowers profusely in spring only. The vigorous plant reaches 15 feet if trained as a climber, but it can be pruned to remain a large shrub. The first of the so-called English roses (see page 56), it is noted for its distinctive fragrance.

CRÉPUSCULE (Noisette; 1904). Orange. See page 34.

TOP TO BOTTOM: Dorothy Perkins, Dortmund, Dublin Bay

DON JUAN (LCL; 1958)

Deep red. Velvety red buds of the best hybrid tea form and size come singly or in small clusters on long stems; flowers open well in all climates. A moderate climber with upright canes that can reach 10 feet, the plant is suitable for use as a pillar-climber. See photo on preceding page.

DOROTHY PERKINS (wichuraiana rambler; 1901)

Rose pink. Late in the spring, phloxlike clusters of small, pompon-shaped blossoms turn the plant into a giant mound of cotton candy. The small, glossy leaves are notoriously mildew prone, but this has no effect on vigor. Virtually identical sports in different colors are 'Lady Godiva' (light pink) and 'White Dorothy'.

DORTMUND (kordesii; 1955)

Bright red. Everything about this rose radiates health and vigor. Clustered single blossoms are cherry red with white centers, displayed against outstanding foliage—dark green, hollylike, and virtually diseaseproof. Use this versatile plant as a climber, a shrub, or even a ground cover.

DR. W. VAN FLEET (LCL; 1910)

Soft pink. Thanks to its *Rosa wichuraiana* ancestry, this plant has unbounded vigor—it's able to cover a large wall or pergola, infiltrate a tree, or simply become an enormous mound that's transformed to an ethereal pink cloud in spring. Glossy foliage provides a backdrop for small clusters of 3-inch, double, cameo pink blossoms. 'New Dawn' (page 81) is a repeat-flowering sport and a smaller grower.

DUBLIN BAY (LCL; 1974)

Bright red. This medium-size climber or pillar-climber (to about 10 feet) seems to glow with health. Foliage is plentiful and deep green; semidouble, velvety bright red flowers come in waves from spring into autumn. The blossoms look like those of a large floribunda or small hybrid tea and open well in virtually all climates.

DYNAMITE (LCL; 1992)

Red. Explosions of dark red, moderately full hybrid tea–style blossoms in small clusters come repeatedly from spring into autumn on an upright pillar-climber to about 10 feet. Foliage is dark green and glossy.

EDEN (Pierre de Ronsard) (LCL; 1987)

Cream and pink. Plump, creamy buds and cupped, pink-blushed open flowers with row upon row of petals have the style of old European roses, but they appear throughout the growing season on a medium-size (8- to 10-foot) climber or pillar-climber with glossy foliage.

FÉLICITÉ ET PERPÉTUE (hybrid sempervirens; 1828)

🌱 Blush white. In one lavish spring flowering, clusters of small pink buds open to perfect rosettes of palest pink fading to white. The extremely vigorous, many-caned plant thrives in sun or shade, growing on walls, on pergolas, or into trees, or even scrambling over the ground. The lovely foliage is nearly evergreen in mild-winter regions.

FRANÇOIS JURANVILLE (wichuraiana rambler; 1906)

🌱 Warm pink. Extremely vigorous (to 20 feet), this many-caned, glossy-leafed plant produces a major springtime show of 2- to 3-inch, coral pink blossoms full of small petals. Sparse repeat bloom may come later in the year.

GARDENIA (wichuraiana rambler; 1899)

🌱 Soft yellow. Small buff yellow buds of perfect hybrid tea style open to blossoms (full-petaled to quartered in form) that age to creamy white. The many-caned plant has smallish leaves that are bronze when new, dark green at maturity. The spring flower show is sometimes is followed by limited repeat bloom, especially in cool-summer regions.

GLOIRE DE DIJON (tea; 1853)

🌱 Yellow blend. The offspring of a tea rose and the Bourbon 'Souvenir de la Malmaison' (see page 33). Plump buds open to very full, rather flat flowers like those of the Bourbon parent, but in a color combination of yellow, pink, and buff. In growth and productivity, the plant resembles a climbing hybrid tea; it often needs time to become established and produce vigorous growth.

Gloire de Dijon

GOLDEN SHOWERS (LCL; 1956)

🌱 Yellow. Although introduced as a pillar-climber, this becomes a moderately large climber (to 12 to 15 feet) in mild climates. Pointed buds of butter yellow open to semidouble, rather ruffled blossoms of a lighter shade; plants are especially free flowering, with handsome glossy leaves. AARS 1956.

HANDEL (LCL; 1965)

🌱 Cream and carmine. Shapely, hybrid tea–style buds swirl open to moderately full, well-formed flowers that offer a striking color contrast: the creamy white petals have deep strawberry pink margins. Use the 10- to 15-foot plant as a climber or pillar-climber; either way, it produces lavish quantities of lovely, long-stemmed blossoms throughout the growing season.

TOP: Félicité et Perpétue   MIDDLE: Golden Showers
BOTTOM LEFT: John Cabot   BOTTOM RIGHT: Handel

HENRY KELSEY (kordesii; 1984)

Red. Brilliant semidouble blossoms with showy yellow stamens appear throughout the growing season on an arching shrub or modest climber to about 10 feet. This is one of the Canadian Explorer roses, developed to withstand southern Canadian winters without protection.

JAUNE DESPREZ (Noisette; 1830). Yellow and pink. See page 35.

JOHN CABOT (kordesii; 1978)

Red. Clustered fully double flowers are borne profusely in spring, sporadically through the rest of the growing season; the light green leaves offer a pleasing contrast to the vivid red blooms. Another of the Canadian Explorer roses (see 'Henry Kelsey'), it can be grown as a modest climber or an arching shrub. See photo on preceding page.

JOSEPH'S COAT (LCL; 1969)

Red, orange, and yellow. Clusters of floribundalike blossoms offer a lovely color change. As the yellow buds expand, the color intensifies to orange; then, with exposure to sunlight, the petals flush with red, until the entire flower is crimson when fully open. Glossy foliage adorns a plant to 12 feet; it can be used as a climber, pillar-climber, or free-standing shrub.

LADY WATERLOW (hybrid tea; 1903)

Soft pink. Nicely tapered buds open to large, moderately full blossoms in blended creamy pink, beautifully set off by exceptional mid-green foliage with elegantly tapered leaflets. The plant is a vigorous grower to about 15 feet.

LAMARQUE (Noisette; 1830). White. See page 35.

LÉONTINE GERVAIS (wichuraiana rambler; 1903)

Apricot blend. In a profuse spring show, small clusters of plump apricot buds unfold to full, 2-inch flowers that age to creamy apricot buff. Glossy green, bronze-tinted leaves clothe long, supple canes to 15 feet.

MARÉCHAL NIEL (Noisette; 1864). Yellow. See page 35.

MERMAID (hybrid bracteata; 1918)

Soft yellow. For mild-winter regions, this unique rose offers single, 4-inch flowers from spring through autumn, scattered across a dense backdrop of light green leaves with a lacquerlike sheen. The ultra-vigorous, thorny plant is suitable for covering walls or pergolas, or even as a giant haystack of a free-standing shrub.

MME. ALFRED CARRIÈRE (Noisette; 1879). Pinkish white. See page 35.

TOP: Joseph's Coat
BOTTOM LEFT: Mermaid   BOTTOM RIGHT: Mme. Grégoire Staechelin

ABOVE: Paul's Himalayan Musk Rambler
BELOW: New Dawn

MME. GRÉGOIRE STAECHELIN (LCL; 1927)

Pink. Great ruffled blossoms—like Victorian artificial flow-ers—bedeck a large (to 20-foot) plant in one extravagant spring flowering. Petals are bright pink on the upper sur-faces, darker pink on the backs. With this rose, it pays *not* to remove spent flowers: large, pear-shaped hips form after bloom, then turn orange in autumn.

NEW DAWN (LCL; 1930)

Light pink. This repeat-flowering, less rampant-growing sport of 'Dr. W. van Fleet' was the first plant to be patented (see "Plant patent" on page 122). It is also the first really cold-tolerant climber with hybrid tea–type blossoms. Glossy dark green leaves are a pleasing foil to the slightly two-tone, silvery soft pink flowers that bloom individually and in small clusters. The vigorous plant reaches about 15 feet and can be used as a climber, pillar-climber, or free-standing shrub.

Paul's Scarlet Climber

PAUL'S HIMALAYAN MUSK RAMBLER (rambler; date unknown)

🐾 Pink. Only for the adventurous gardener with large grounds! This is a rose to elicit gasps of disbelief and admiration: relatively slender canes easily grow to 30 feet, ascending trees, covering outbuildings, or simply making a huge haystack of growth. In spring, pendent clusters of small, blush pink rosettes engulf the plant in a haze of color. See photo on preceding page.

PAUL'S SCARLET CLIMBER (LCL; 1916)

🐾 Bright red. Until repeat-flowering 'Blaze' came along, this was *the* red climber for springtime mass display. Clusters of double blossoms in brilliant, unfading scarlet cover the vigorous medium-size plant over a long period in spring. It's equally good trained on a fence or ascending a post.

PIÑATA (LCL; 1978)

🐾 Yellow and orange. Glossy foliage sets off floribunda-style,
🐾 golden yellow flowers edged and washed in orange red. Growth is restrained (to 8 to 10 feet) and somewhat shrubby; the plant is best used as a pillar-climber or shrub.

POLKA (LCL; 1992)

🐾 Orange apricot. From plump orange buds, petals unfold and expand into large, full, gracefully waved blossoms of golden, peachy apricot. Glossy light green leaves cover a vigorous climber to 12 feet.

RÊVE D'OR (Noisette; 1869). Golden apricot. See page 35.
ROSA BANKSIAE (species). White or yellow. See page 16.
ROSA LAEVIGATA (species). White. See page 17.

ROYAL GOLD (LCL; 1957)

🐾 Deep yellow. Glowing yellow buds of hybrid tea form and size come on a stiff-caned plant that's a pillar-climber in colder regions, a moderate climber to about 10 feet in mild-winter areas. Coming individually or in small clusters, the shapely blossoms fade only slightly as they age.

Royal Gold

ROYAL SUNSET (LCL; 1960)

Orange blend. Shapely buds of hybrid tea elegance are predominantly orange; as the flowers open, sunset tones take over, leading to a final phase of buff apricot or creamy peach. Dark bronzy green, glossy leaves come on a stiff-caned plant to 10 feet; grow it as a modest climber or a large shrub.

Royal Sunset

SOMBREUIL (LCL; date unknown)

Creamy white. Usually catalogued as a climbing tea rose, this plant is neither a tea nor the actual rose 'Sombreuil' (a 19th-century tea rose now rediscovered). By any name, however, it's a superlative climber, rather like 'New Dawn' in foliage and habit. Short, plump buds open to flat, circular, creamy white flowers intricately packed with countless petals; the blossoms are sometimes flushed pink, and they fade to white in the sun. The 10- to 15-foot plant can be trained as a climber or pillar-climber.

VEILCHENBLAU (multiflora rambler; 1909)

Violet blend. The most widely available of several "blue ramblers" (others are 'Bleu Magenta' and 'Violette'), this one has elongated clusters of small, semidouble flowers that open a deep violet color, then fade to nearly gray; the petals are sometimes streaked with white. Plenty of glossy apple green foliage appears on canes that are nearly thornless.

WHITE DAWN (LCL; 1949)

White. This child of 'New Dawn' features ruffled, pure white, semidouble blossoms with the purity and scent of gardenias. A lavish spring display is followed by moderate bloom during summer, then another big burst in autumn. Glossy foliage covers a vigorous plant to about 12 feet; use it as a climber or a free-standing shrub.

WILLIAM BAFFIN (kordesii; 1983)

Deep pink. Semidouble carmine pink blossoms appear in large clusters throughout the growing season on a plant with disease-resistant foliage. One of the hardy Canadian Explorer roses (see 'Henry Kelsey'), it can be grown as a modest climber (to 12 feet) or a large, arching shrub.

ZÉPHIRINE DROUHIN (Bourbon; 1868). Deep pink. See page 33.

TOP: Sombreuil
BOTTOM: William Baffin

The development of miniature roses has waxed and waned over the years, but never has enthusiasm for them been greater than it is today: almost half the new roses registered

MINIATURE
ROSES

each year are miniatures. These little roses offer the full range of hybrid tea color, and some mimic hybrid tea bloom quality. You'll also find smaller versions of shrub and old garden roses, climbers, and ground covers.

Most miniature roses are available by mail from specialty growers; a few appear in standard retail outlets, and some even turn up in supermarkets as flowering pot plants. The varieties profiled in the following six pages are a selection of new and old favorites; all have been given the highest ratings by the American Rose Society.

Though all miniatures are small, they do vary. Some have tiny leaves and 1-inch blossoms; others have larger leaves and 3-inch, hybrid tea–style flowers that blur the line between miniature and floribunda. Overall plant size varies, too, and may or may not correspond to the size of leaf and bloom; the most miniature leaves and blossoms don't always come on the shortest plants.

Unless otherwise stated, all the miniatures described here are repeat blooming. Foliage is described when it is worthy of note.

They may be small, but miniature roses
light up the garden with color during the growing season.

Cupcake

Each of the following descriptions includes a code letter signifying the height of the variety when grown in the ground: S (plant reaches about 1 foot high); M (1 to 2 feet); T (over 2 feet). The letters AARS at the end of an entry indicate that the rose has received the All-America Rose Selection Award (see page 123); the letters AoE mean it has received the Award of Excellence from the American Rose Society, based on high scores in trials conducted over a 2-year period in test gardens throughout the United States.

ADAM'S SMILE (1991)

Dark pink. Elegant, pointed buds unfurl to full blossoms with petals that roll back at the margins to create pointed petal tips. The deep pink flowers, their petal backs infused with yellow, are carried against a background of dark, glossy foliage. M.

AMERICAN ROSE CENTENNIAL (1991)

Cream and pink. Graceful, pointed buds on long stems swirl open to full flowers of creamy ivory, each petal margined in soft pink. The plant is vigorous and free flowering. T.

BEAUTY SECRET (1965)

Red. Lovely long, pointed buds open to semidouble, cherry red blossoms with pointed petal tips. The plant is upright and bushy, with dark green foliage. M. AoE 1975.

BLACK JADE (1985)

Darkest red. Dusky deep red—almost black—buds of the best hybrid tea form open to full, fairly large blossoms of velvety dark red. The flowers come singly and in clusters. M. AoE 1985.

CAL POLY (1991)

Yellow. Brilliant color and ease of growth are the selling points for this one. Against a dense backdrop of dark green leaves, the pointed buds open to moderately full flowers. M. AoE 1992.

CARROT TOP (1994)

Orange. From attractive buds to fully double blooms, this scaled-down replica of a hybrid tea blazes a clear, pure orange. The bushy plant is clothed in dark, leathery leaves. M.

CHILD'S PLAY (1991)

White and pink. The child who could color these elegant hybrid tea–style blooms would have to wield the crayons carefully: each broad white petal has a precise edging of delicate pink. The plant is vigorous and free blooming. M. AoE and AARS 1993.

CINDERELLA (1953)

White. Suitably tiny leaves provide the background for tiny, shapely buds that open to very double, 1-inch flowers. In cool weather, the blossoms may be pale pink. S.

CUDDLES (1978)

Coral pink. Shapely orange-pink buds open to full blossoms in a paler shade, with the best hybrid tea shape. The upright-growing bush has dark green foliage. M. AoE 1979.

Beauty Secret

Black Jade

Child's Play

CUPCAKE (1981)

Pink. The buds and very full open blossoms, both in a clear cotton-candy pink, show the finest hybrid tea style. Plenty of glossy foliage completes the picture. M. AoE 1983.

DEE BENNETT (1988)

Apricot blend. Shapely buds in an orange-tinted yellow open to full blossoms in a blending of lighter shades. The plant is bushy, with dark, glossy foliage. T. AoE 1989.

DREAMGLO (1978)

White and red. Hybrid tea–type buds and very full flowers (some in clusters, some on individual stems) appear on vigorous, upright-growing plants. The blossoms offer a dramatic color contrast: the petals are white, edged and washed in red. T.

FIGURINE (1991)

Ivory and pink. Borne individually on long stems, the long, pointed buds and full open blooms have the smooth delicacy of fine porcelain. The petals are ivory, washed in softest pink. M. AoE 1992.

FIREWORKS (1992)

Yellow and red. Opening from plump buds, the moderately full blossoms look lit from within: the bright yellow petals are brushed with brilliant scarlet over much of the upper surfaces, and near the margins on the backs. The plant is bushy and compact. M.

GOLDEN HALO (1991)

Yellow. Blossoms of a bright, buttery yellow appear nonstop on a vigorous, bushy plant with distinctive dark, textured leaves. M. AoE 1991.

GOOD MORNING AMERICA (1991)

Yellow. Lovely buds and full, pleasantly fragrant blooms are borne individually on cutting-length stems. The yellow color is clear and unshaded in cool conditions, lightly brushed with red when the weather is sunny and warm. M. AoE 1991.

GOURMET POPCORN (1986)

White. This sport of 'Popcorn' is a puffed-up version with larger flowers of the same pure white on a notably larger plant. The rangy, spreading bush is almost always cloaked in clusters of 1-inch blooms; it's attractive spilling over the edge of a large container or hanging basket. T.

Dreamglo   Green Ice

GREEN ICE (1971)

Greenish white. Pink-tinted white buds open to informal, ruffled blossoms that turn to soft, pale green as they mature (though they may retain pink tinges). The plant is mounding and spreading, useful in hanging baskets. M.

HAPPY TRAILS (1993)

Pink. Large clusters of bright pink, pomponlike blossoms seem to burst from a spreading mound of small, bright green leaves—in fact, the blooms are so abundant that the stems bend beneath their weight, making 'Happy Trails' a good choice for a raised planter, container, or hanging basket. S.

HEARTBREAKER (1990)

White and pink. The large blossoms, each carried at the end of a long stem with glossy leaves, are perfect replicas of hybrid tea blooms. The petals are white, with raspberry pink brushed inward from the edges. T.

HOT TAMALE (1993)

Orange blend. Small clusters of large, hybrid tea–form flowers start with shapely yellow buds; as these unfold, the petal surfaces show a blend of orange and pink, while the undersides remain largely yellow. The bush is dark foliaged and somewhat spreading. T. AoE 1994.

IRRESISTIBLE (1990)

Pinkish white. Long-stemmed, long-budded blossoms suggest a small version of the hybrid tea 'Pristine' (page 50): they're a satiny ivory white, tinged ever so slightly with pink and centered with blush pink. The upright-growing plant is a profuse bloomer. T.

Gourmet Popcorn

JEAN KENNEALLY (1984)

Apricot. Elegant, pointed buds open slowly to semidouble flowers that are always shapely. The plant is vigorous and free flowering. T. AoE 1986.

JENNIFER (1985)

Pink and white. Shapely buds are white—but as the blossoms unfurl, you see more and more of the soft lavender pink on the petal surfaces. The vigorous plant is quick to repeat bloom, with each flush of flowering soon followed by another. T. AoE 1985.

JUDY FISCHER (1968)

Rose pink. Beautifully formed buds open to blossoms of about half-dollar size, each a perfect hybrid tea replica. Bloom is plentiful throughout the growing season on a plant with bronze-tinged dark green foliage. M. AoE 1975.

KRISTIN (1992)

White and red. As the lovely urn-shaped buds slowly unfold, they reveal a color contrast: each white petal has a broad margin of carmine red. These faultless flowers are borne individually on long stems. T. AoE 1993.

LAVENDER JEWEL (1978)

Lavender. The plump hybrid tea–style buds and full, fragrant, 1-inch blossoms are soft lavender, tinged with magenta on the petal edges. The plant is bushy and compact. M.

LITTLE ARTIST (1982)

Red and white. The semidouble, ruffled, vibrant red flowers have striking white centers and white petal backs. The plant is rounded, with glossy, notably disease-resistant foliage. M.

LITTLE JACKIE (1982)

Orange and yellow. Glossy foliage provides a pleasing background for a combination of bright colors: the shapely buds and fragrant, moderately full blossoms are sherbet orange with yellow petal backs. M. AoE 1984.

Magic Carrousel

CLOCKWISE FROM TOP LEFT: Jean Kenneally, Little Artist, Minnie Pearl, Little Jackie

LOVING TOUCH (1983)

Apricot. Urn-shaped apricot buds open to 3-inch, moderately double blooms of a smooth, creamy apricot. The spreading bush produces plenty of flowers. T. AoE 1985.

MAGIC CARROUSEL (1972)

White and red. From the buds to the open blooms, this one offers an impressive color contrast: at every stage, you clearly see the white petals' precise cherry red margins. The flowers come singly and in clusters on a vigorous, free-blooming plant. T. AoE 1975.

MARY MARSHALL (1970)

Orange blend. Flawless orange buds unfurl to fairly large flowers showing tints of red and yellow. The leaves are small and leathery. M. AoE 1975.

MILLIE WALTERS (1983)

Coral pink. The buds are dark coral, the full blossoms a paler shade. Both buds and open blooms are perfect miniatures of the best hybrid tea flowers. T.

MINNIE PEARL (1982)

Coral pink blend. Long, shapely buds of a soft, ivory-infused coral pink swirl open to full blossoms that darken a bit in sunshine. M.

CLOCKWISE FROM TOP LEFT: Orange Honey, Orange Sunblaze, Popcorn, Peaches 'n' Cream

ORANGE SUNBLAZE (1981)

Orange red. Carried in clusters on a free-blooming plant, the full, rosette-shaped blossoms are a clear, vibrant bright orange that verges on red. The bush is compact and symmetrical, good for foreground border plantings. M. (There is also a climbing sport that reaches about 6 feet.)

PACESETTER (1979)

White. Perfect long, tapered buds swirl open to very full, crystalline blossoms that are usually carried individually on long stems. The plant is upright, with dark green foliage. M. AoE 1981.

PARTY GIRL (1979)

Pink blend. Plump, shapely buds of yellow- or cream-tinged apricot open to small, moderately double blossoms flushed with salmon pink. M. AoE 1981.

PEACHES 'N' CREAM (1976)

Pride 'n' Joy

Pink blend. Beautiful buds and large (for a miniature rose) blossoms offer hybrid tea perfection in soft pink with ivory shadings. This one isn't as quick to repeat bloom as most other miniatures. M. AoE 1977.

POPCORN (1973)

White. Like a popper full of popcorn, the full, bushy plant bursts with bloom, bearing clusters of small, globular buds and dime-size, semidouble white flowers with butter yellow stamens. M.

MOTHER'S LOVE (1989)

Pink and yellow blend. Elegant buds and broad-petaled, 3-inch flowers show off a smooth, creamy blend of soft yellow, pink, and coral; the colors are darker in cool weather. The plant is vigorous and spreading. M.

OLD GLORY (1988)

Red. Picture a perfect red hybrid tea blossom reduced to 2½ inches wide: that's 'Old Glory'. Plenty of these richly colored blossoms come on a vigorous bush with dark, disease-resistant foliage. M. AoE 1988.

ORANGE HONEY (1979)

Yellow and orange blend. Moderately double, informal blossoms start as golden orange buds; as these open, the petals reveal softer pink and orange shades on their upper surfaces. All these colors are at their brightest in cooler weather. The mounding, spreading plant is attractive grown in a hanging basket. M.

Rainbow's End

PRIDE 'N' JOY (1991)

Orange and yellow. Fat buds open to moderately full blossoms in a vivid combination of bright orange with yellow shading on the petal backs. The strong-growing plant is covered in matte green foliage. T. AARS 1992.

RAINBOW'S END (1984)

Yellow and red. Shapely yellow buds are touched red on the petal tips; as the full blossoms unfold, the red color appears at the petal edges (more so in sunshine, much less in shade and when skies are overcast). Glossy leaves complete the picture. M. AoE 1986.

RISE 'N' SHINE (1977)

Yellow. Beautifully shaped buds and full flowers glow like early morning sunshine on a vigorous, free-flowering bush with excellent foliage. AoE 1978.

SANTA CLAUS (1994)

Dark red. No white beard here (and no white cuffs or collar either)—just the basic red of Santa's outfit. Tapered, deep red buds and velvety, moderately full flowers are complemented by glossy dark green foliage with elongated leaflets. T.

SNOW BRIDE (1982)

White. Creamy buds of perfect hybrid tea form, carried both individually and in small clusters on long stems, open to pure white, moderately full, lightly fragrant blossoms. M. AoE 1983.

Winsome

TOP LEFT AND BOTTOM: Rise 'n' Shine   TOP RIGHT: Starina

STARINA (1965)

Orange red. This one is a classic, its glossy dark leaves framing faultless buds and blossoms that truly are hybrid teas in miniature. M.

SWEET CHARIOT (1984)

Violet. Low and spreading when planted in the ground, it cascades gracefully if grown in a container or hanging basket. Clusters of tiny, full, grape-purple blossoms have a strong, sweet perfume. L.

TEXAS (1984)

Yellow. Sunny hybrid tea–style blossoms come singly and in small clusters, borne above glossy leaves on an upright plant. T.

WINSOME (1984)

Lavender blend. Adorning a large, vigorous, dark-foliaged plant are perfect hybrid tea–form blossoms in blended tones of lilac, magenta, and purple. T. AoE 1985.

CLIMBING MINIATURES

CANDY CANE (1958)

Pink and white. Deep pink blossoms striped in white suggested this variety's name. Clusters of these lively semi-double blooms decorate a large-leafed, arching plant that climbs to about 4 feet.

JEANNE LAJOIE (1975)

Medium pink. Bountiful clusters of shapely buds open to very double, 2-inch blossoms, making this versatile plant a bright spot in the garden. Train it as a climber, use it as a hedge, or just let it develop as an arching shrub. The canes reach 6 to 10 feet. AoE 1977.

NOZOMI (1968)

White. The major bloom season comes in spring, when the lax, glossy-foliaged, 5-foot-long canes are spangled with single blossoms. Use the plant as a climber, a ground cover, or a trailing decoration for a retaining wall.

ORCHID JUBILEE (1993)

Lavender. Clusters of fluffy, pinkish lavender blossoms slightly more than an inch across adorn a vigorous, fairly upright-growing plant. Let it climb to about 6 feet, or use it as an arching shrub.

RADIANT (1988)

Orange. Brilliant color, attractive shape, and powerfully sweet perfume—this variety's blossoms offer all three. The 6-foot plant is outfitted in dark, moderately glossy foliage.

RED CASCADE (1976)

Bright red. The name describes the effect it gives when grown in a hanging basket—but this 5-foot, lax-caned plant can be grown as a climber, too, its clusters of 1-inch blossoms making just as bright a display. AoE 1976.

SNOWFALL (1988)

White. Clusters of small, well-formed flowers lavishly adorn a glossy-leafed climber with canes reaching 8 to 12 feet long.

TWISTER (1997)

Red and white. This 5-foot climber offers an eye-popping display of 1½-inch blossoms decked out in red and white stripes. They're very double, with pointed petal tips—a shape that makes them look more like dahlias then roses.

WORK OF ART (1989)

Orange blend. Coral, orange, and yellow mingle in hybrid tea–style blossoms on cutting-length stems. The canes reach about 6 feet long.

Work of Art

TOP: Jeanne Lajoie   BOTTOM: Nozomi

There's no mystery to growing roses. Success simply involves learning the plants' basic needs, understanding the advantages and liabilities of your garden environment, and then

THE ART OF GROWING
ROSES

adjusting the care you provide to suit your particular conditions. It's no secret, of course, that doing the job well requires some work and attention. But having great roses entails no more labor (and may even require less) than maintaining a lawn or planting an annual vegetable garden.

In this chapter, you'll learn the essentials of growing roses, from tips on choosing the best plants and selecting good planting sites to the details of year-round care. You will also find instructions on cutting flowers for indoor decoration—surely a fitting reward for your outdoor labors. And if you have truly been bitten by the rose bug, you'll appreciate the directions for starting your own plants on pages 118–120.

A riot of roses billowing from a profusion of perennials is opulent
testament to the value of proper siting and good care.

WHERE TO PLANT ROSES

Technically speaking, all roses are flowering shrubs. Yet members of the group vary widely, from miniatures under a foot tall to climbing sorts that consider a 50-foot tree no obstacle. Such variety yields a wealth of choices, offering vibrant flower color from spring to frost (even year-round, in frost-free climates), an assortment of foliage textures and hues, and even sparkling autumn displays of bright fruits.

Narrowing the multitude of possible selections to just those that will thrive in your garden starts with learning the conditions roses need for a first-rate performance. Once you know these essentials, you'll also know what parts of your garden are naturally congenial to roses. You can then begin the enjoyable task of choosing the roses you want.

WHAT ROSES LIKE

Choose the right location at the start! Once established, roses dislike transplanting—and the process becomes more laborious as time passes and plants grow larger. Keep the following points in mind as you consider planting sites.

EXPOSURE is crucial to success. Roses flourish in sunny locations. Most need at least 6 hours of sunshine daily, preferably all morning long and into the afternoon. Where weather is consistently cool or overcast, give roses a location that's in full sun all day; where summer heat is intense, choose a spot that receives filtered sunlight during the hottest afternoon hours. Certain roses, including some old garden types, shrub roses (especially the hybrid musks), and climbers, are noted for their ability to thrive in partial shade. Shaded locations still should receive plenty of light, though; dense shade hinders growth and encourages foliage diseases.

Avoid planting roses where wind constantly buffets the plants. Continuous strong winds spoil flowers and cause rapid transpiration from leaves, obliging you to water more often.

SOIL should be both moisture retentive and fast draining. See pages 100–101 for guidelines on preparing soil for planting. If improving the native soil is too daunting a task, consider creating raised beds which you can fill with rose-friendly soil.

Note: A condition known as "specific replant disease" inhibits growth of new roses planted in soil where roses have

Whatever the setting, roses turn in the best performance if given a sunny location.

already been established. If you want to plant new roses in soil where roses have been growing for 5 years or more, dig planting holes 1½ feet deep and at least that wide; then replace the old soil with fresh soil taken from another part of the garden.

WATER must be available throughout the growing season. A steady supply of water and nutrients produces healthy, vigorous plants. If you plan to include roses among other shrubs or to plant them close to shrubs or trees, avoid companions that have greedy surface roots; if subjected to aggressive competition for water and fertilizer, your roses will suffer. For more on watering and watering systems, see pages 104–106.

PLANNING THE PLANTING

There are so many enticing roses that you may be tempted to buy every one that sounds appealing, then crowd them all into a single sunny planting. This would teach you a valuable (if painful) lesson: to grow well and look good, roses need a certain amount of elbow room. To avoid the disappointment that overcrowding brings, plan ahead for the kind of planting you want, then choose only as many plants as will thrive in the available space (see "Layout and Spacing," page 96).

EXCLUSIVELY ROSES. An area given over to roses alone is a long-standing tradition for showcasing hybrid teas, grandifloras, and (to a lesser extent) floribundas. The more formal rose gardens are laid out in rows of military precision, sometimes with standard ("tree") roses to add height and stress the formality; each bed is separated from the next by pathways of lawn or paving. To introduce some informality, let the beds move in flowing curves to produce irregular shapes; to soften the effect further, add shrub and old garden roses and climbers, with miniature types at the garden's margins.

An all-rose planting is an efficient setup for a cutting garden and accommodates the most roses in a given area—a particular advantage for the enthusiast with space constraints.

ROSES IN PARTNERSHIP. Viewed as flowering shrubs, roses are valuable if not indispensable components of mixed floral plantings. And the modern mixed border—a descendant of the old-fashioned cottage garden, in which everything from blooming shrubs to vegetables assorted in riotous profusion—offers niches for roses of all sorts.

The more vigorous hybrid teas bring cutting-quality flowers to mixed plantings of annuals, perennials, and other flowering shrubs. But the most valuable roses for such gardens are the species and old garden roses, shrub roses, climbers, and miniatures. Including both spring and repeat bloomers, these groups offer a great variety of flower, foliage, and plant styles; some put on a show even after bloom time is past, bearing colorful hips to enliven the autumn scene.

Roses suit almost any garden style. The formal planting (BELOW LEFT) is a traditional showcase; in a cottage garden, roses may be used as accents (BELOW RIGHT) or repeated elements (BOTTOM).

Just one kind of rose, on its own or in a group, makes a striking garden statement—from informal shrub (TOP LEFT) or carefully trained pillar-climber (TOP RIGHT) to a chorus line of standards (BOTTOM; shown here is 'Summer Fashion', page 70).

SPECIALTY PLANTINGS. Roses can shine in solo acts. Carefully chosen and sited, an individual rose makes an unforgettable accent. A single shrub rose provides a colorful welcome beside a gate or entryway; just one climbing rose can transform an arch, pergola, or rail fence; one of the extra-vigorous sorts adds unexpected decoration to a tall-growing tree. A judiciously placed standard rose is an immediate focal point.

Mass plantings of a single variety offer another unusual way to present roses. Shrub types and some of the old European sorts make surprisingly good informal hedges of various heights. Larger growers serve as background and barrier plants; lower-growing types define spaces within a garden. To border a path-

way with color from spring until autumn, look no farther than the miniatures.

LAYOUT AND SPACING

Roses perform best when uncrowded, and providing routine care is simplest when the plants are accessible from all or most sides. But what counts as generous spacing in one climate may constitute crowding in another. Follow the guidelines below to set up a planting that will be both easy to maintain and a pleasure to view.

DESIGN FOR MAINTENANCE. Recognize that all roses need pruning, fertilizing, and occasional attention to pest control. Whether you plant your roses on their own or use them in mixed plantings, it's best to make the beds narrow enough to let you reach the plants in the center from either side. This allows you to maintain the planting without having to wade into it. In an all-rose setting, beds should be no wider than three bushes across; in a bed against a fence or wall, two bushes deep is best. When plants are laid out in parallel rows, care is simpler if the spacing is staggered.

SPACE BY CLIMATE. Relative spacing is more or less constant: the average miniatures are planted closer together than are shrub roses. But the exact distance between plants depends on how large those roses will become in your climate.

Where winter cold kills canes down to their protection and the growing season lasts just 3 to 4 months, roses seldom achieve the bulk they do in warmer regions. Spaced 2 to 2½ feet apart, hybrid teas and grandifloras will fill in a bed without tangling. But in the warmer parts of the West, Southwest, and South, the same plants grow larger and need about 3-foot spacing. Where there's little or no frost to enforce winter dormancy (as in much of Florida, the Gulf Coast, California, and parts of Arizona), roses grow so prodigiously all year that the hybrid teas and grandifloras need to be planted at least 4 feet apart.

Floribundas usually grow smaller than hybrid teas and should be planted correspondingly closer: 1½ to 2 feet apart in the coldest regions, 2 to 2½ feet apart in moderately cold areas, about 3 feet apart where winters are mild.

Despite the name, miniature roses include varieties that, in mild climates, can grow to 3 feet high and wide in a single year. For mass effect, plant the smaller-growing miniatures from 1 to 1½ feet apart; larger-growing types appreciate a spacing of 2 to 3 feet. Use the closer spacings for colder climates, the wider ones in regions where winters are milder.

Most rose species, shrub roses, and old garden types need more room to expand than do modern hybrid teas, grandifloras, floribundas, and miniatures. Exactly how far apart to plant depends on the growth habit of the particular variety. In general, allow 5 to 6 feet between plants where winters are cold, up to twice that much space in the mildest areas. In any climate, allow a bit more room for types with long, arching canes.

What better, more pleasurable way to choose roses than to visit a garden featuring many types and colors? Public rose gardens offer the opportunity to admire and browse, as do some commercial growers' display gardens (ABOVE).

SHOPPING FOR ROSES

Choosing roses is a pleasure surpassed only by the delight of seeing them growing and blooming in the garden. The selection process can seem overwhelming, however. When you see the dozens of color photographs that beckon from catalogs, magazines, books, and nursery labels, your first reaction may be: "so many roses, so little space!" At this point, a bit of study will help guide you through the wealth of offerings.

NARROWING THE FIELD

First, decide which sorts of roses you want to grow. Do you want sophisticated modern hybrid teas for garden and indoor ornament, or historic roses for a connection to times past? Do you need roses that are essentially flowering shrubs? Do you want foreground or background plants? Perhaps all you want are roses for containers on your patio, in which case you'll find a dazzling array among miniature varieties alone. And what about climbers to clamber over a pergola, climb a tree, or festoon a rail fence?

Once you've identified the general categories you need, you can address the most important question: which individual varieties will perform best in your climate? Local growers can offer plenty of advice on this score, and even a chat with the neighbors is likely to yield a limited list of sure performers (usually hybrid teas). If there's a public garden nearby—or better yet, a public *rose* garden—visit it during the bloom season for a first-hand look. Check for plant vigor and resistance to foliage diseases; note which varieties fail to open well, open too rapidly, or fade to unattractive colors.

Lacking first-hand or anecdotal information, you can rely to some extent on awards and ratings. National awards and high ratings will tell you that the rose has succeeded in a variety of regions with varied growing conditions and is therefore likely to give a fair to good performance in your garden. Low ratings and/or lack of awards, however, don't universally condemn a rose: because ratings are averages, there's a chance that a lower-ranked variety may be a stellar performer in your climate.

WHERE TO BUY ROSES

It's easy to buy roses—they're sold in mail-order catalogs, in nurseries and garden centers, in home improvement and hardware stores, and even in some supermarkets. With careful shopping, you can buy good plants from any of these outlets.

MAIL-ORDER SPECIALISTS are convenient. You do all your shopping from home, and the selection is often greater than that offered by retail outlets. And if you're looking for roses other than mainstream hybrid teas, grandifloras, and floribundas, mail-order is practically the only way to shop. It's true that you can't personally choose the plants, but reputable suppliers are careful to send out good-quality stock, since their existence depends on satisfied customers. Most mail-order purveyors of dormant roses for winter planting send out their catalogs in summer or early autumn, well in advance of actual planting time; it's best to order as early as possible, while stocks are still ample. If the grower ships small roses growing in containers, the catalog will tell you when the plants are mailed out. Such plants do best if set out in early to midspring, giving them a full growing season to become established. In mild-winter regions, young roses may also be planted in autumn; they'll put out roots during the cool, moist winter months.

NURSERIES AND GARDEN CENTERS give you the chance to select plants in person: bare-root in the dormant season, planted in containers during the rest of the year. These outlets are likely to offer the current best-sellers and time-tested favorites, but they usually don't sell an extensive array of varieties. Some local nurseries make a point of offering varieties that do especially well in your area, whether or not they are widely sold elsewhere.

NON-NURSERY OUTLETS often are more accessible than nurseries simply because they are more numerous—and during the dormant season, many suddenly burst into "bloom" with bare-root roses. The plants tend to be current award winners and established favorites; you're also likely to encounter some decidedly older favorites (those considered hot stuff in the '40s, for example) and seldom-catalogued varieties. If you have the impulse to buy, do so as soon as possible after the roses are put on display, since the plants are often kept in less than ideal conditions: indoors in warm, dry air, or outdoors at the mercy of wind, sun, and daily temperature swings. Nor can you be sure that the roses are cared for by plant-wise staff. The longer these plants remain on the shelf, the greater the chances they will suffer some deterioration.

HOW ROSES ARE GROWN

Roses for garden planting are sold throughout the year. During the dormant season, bare-root plants dominate the market. In the warmer months, plants in containers are available from retail outlets and even some mail-order firms.

BARE-ROOT PLANTS have been tended in commercial growing fields for 1 to 2 years, then dug and supplied to retailers (or offered by mail-order) with their roots bare of soil but kept moist enough to prevent dehydration. Retail nurseries may hold bare-root stock in beds of damp sawdust, allowing you to pull

A well-stocked retail nursery becomes a rose garden during the flowering period, letting you purchase your favorites in bloom for immediate planting.

During the dormant season, you'll find bare-root roses ready for planting in retail nurseries and garden centers (LEFT). In the growing season, blooming roses in containers (RIGHT) attract potential buyers.

the plants out and scrutinize roots as well as canes. Many nurseries, garden centers, and non-nursery outlets present bare-root roses partially bagged: the roots are enclosed in long, narrow bags containing moist, sawdustlike material, while the canes are on view—sometimes enclosed in plastic to conserve moisture, sometimes exposed. Occasionally, you may find plants having wax-coated canes—again, a hedge against dehydration. One supplier even offers bare-root roses "planted" in paper boxes of soil; you just dig a hole and plant the entire box.

ROSES IN CONTAINERS will entice you during bloom time in nurseries and garden centers. You can judge flowers, foliage, and overall health at a glance, but you'll rarely find an extensive selection, since the plants are often potted-up leftovers from bare-root season. For the widest possible choice and best plant condition, shop for containerized roses during the first flowering flush of spring. In most cases (miniatures and some shrub or ground cover types are exceptions), look for plants growing in large (3- to 5-gallon) containers; if pots are this big, it's unlikely that the roots were pruned to fit the containers.

A number of mail-order specialty growers offer own-root plants (see below) in smaller containers through much of the year. Like larger plants in larger containers, these are best purchased for planting early in the growing season.

ROSE PLANTS: BUDDED AND OWN-ROOT

All roses have roots, of course—but roots and plant may or may not naturally belong together. *Own-root plants* are grown from cuttings: both roots *and* canes of a given variety belong to that variety. *Budded plants* are a union of two roses: canes belong to one rose (the variety you purchase), roots to another. What are the differences?

BUDDED PLANTS begin life as cuttings of selected sorts known to produce good root systems; these are known as the *understock*. After the understock cuttings have rooted, growth buds (sometimes called "growth eyes") of the desired flowering variety are inserted into them; once a bud has formed a union with the understock, all understock above the bud is cut off, letting the bud grow. After a year or more, you have a full-size plant ready for sale.

Budded plants have a commercial advantage. Root systems of a given understock are uniform, and certain understocks have been developed (or discovered) that produce particularly well-balanced root systems—flexible (good for packing and shipping) and able to produce a sizable plant in a year or two. Some roses, primarily certain hybrid teas, are stronger growing and more productive as budded plants. And a few (gallicas are a prime example) have better plant form when budded: the budded plant develops into a recognizable

bush with all canes springing from a single point, whereas own-root plants tend to colonize into spreading clumps of stems. One disadvantage of budded roses: if top growth is killed but roots survive, regrowth will be of the understock. In a small percentage of cases, the understock will send up canes while its budded component is growing; if not removed, these growths ("suckers") can overwhelm the budded rose.

OWN-ROOT PLANTS eliminate the budding step. Cuttings of the desired varieties are planted; each variety grows on its own roots. The majority of roses grow well on their own roots—often as well as budded plants, though they may take a bit longer to become full-size bushes. Own-root root systems vary from one rose to another: some are as well-balanced as those of budded plants, while others are distinctly lopsided or stiff. Many historic and shrub roses are sold as own-root plants, as are virtually all miniatures.

Budded rose (LEFT); own-root rose (RIGHT)

SOILS AND PLANTING

Growing roses starts with groundwork. Begin by determining your soil's characteristics, including its assets and possible shortcomings. Then complete any necessary improvements before you plant.

SOIL BASICS

All soils are composed of mineral particles formed by the natural breakdown of rock. But there's more to it than that: what appears to be an inert mass is really a lively, complex environment that also contains air, water, organic matter, and a variety of organisms, from earthworms to bacteria. It's the balance of all these components that determines each soil's character and quality.

One very important aspect of soil quality is *drainage*. Water applied to the soil surface percolates down through the pore spaces between soil particles. At first, it completely fills the pores. In time, though, it is drawn away—by gravity (which pulls it further downward), by plant roots (which absorb it), and by wind and heat (which cause it to evaporate both from the soil surface and through plant leaves). As water leaves the pores, air returns to them, until just a film of water (unavailable to roots) remains on soil particles.

Check drainage by filling a test hole with water, then clocking the time needed for absorption.

In clay soils—popularly known as "heavy" soils—the particles are minute, flattened grains that group together tightly (rather like a pile of playing cards), producing a compact mass with microscopic pore spaces. Drainage tends to be slow: water and nutrients percolate through the tiny pores very slowly, and air space is limited. On the plus side, slower drainage allows you to water and fertilize less often; on the minus side, clay is difficult for roots to penetrate, and in rainy periods it can remain saturated and airless, to the point of rotting roots. In spring, clay soils warm slowly.

Sandy soils (so-called "light" soils) are at the other end of the spectrum. They have large, irregularly rounded particles that assort something like marbles in a jar, with large pore spaces that allow freer exchange of moisture and air. Roots growing in sandy soils run virtually no risk of being waterlogged. It's keep-

ing them moist that's the problem: if you garden in sand, you'll need to water frequently. Fertilizing is required more often as well, since the necessary frequent waterings leach nutrients away. Sandy soils are the first to warm in spring.

Most garden soils fall somewhere between the clay/sand extremes just described. The best ones contain a mixture of particle sizes and shapes, balancing the density of clay with the permeability of sand. To determine whether your garden soil tends toward clay or sand, try a few simple tests.

First, just look at the soil: if it has a high clay content, it will usually crack when dry. Second, perform a touch test. Moist clay soil feels slick to the touch; if you squeeze a ball of it hard in your hand, it will ooze through your fingers in ribbons. Sandy soil, in contrast, feels gritty. If you compress it in your hand, it forms a ball that breaks apart at the slightest prod.

Third, test for for drainage—a good indication of a soil's composition. Dig a hole about 1½ feet deep in the area where you want to plant, then fill it with water. If water remains in the hole after about 8 hours, the soil has poor drainage and is probably clayey in nature (but see also "Compacted soil" and "Shallow soil" under "Problem Soils" on the facing page).

IMPROVING SOIL

Roses need regular moisture for best growth, but their roots will not thrive in poorly drained soil that remains saturated and airless for any length of time. If your current garden soil grows good vegetables (or crops of husky weeds!), it will probably grow good roses just as it is. But any soil can be improved, and some soils actually need such improvement if roses are to flourish.

Organic matter—including compost, peat moss, nitrogen-fortified wood by-products, and a host of other choices—is the all-purpose soil amendment. In clay, organic matter literally forces the soil structure apart: the tiny particles become grouped into larger aggregates, and water penetrates more easily. In sandy soils, organic material becomes lodged in the relatively

---

RAISED BEDS

The obstacles of shallow or poorly drained soil can be overcome by constructing raised beds. The principle is simple: you put decent soil on top of the existing soil, blend the two together, and achieve enough depth to satisfy rose roots. To form the sides of the beds and keep soil in place, use decay-resistant wood, landscape timbers, brick, concrete block, or even stone. Plan to have the soil surface within the raised bed 1 foot or more above the normal grade outside. Dig organic materials into the upper 1½ to 2 feet of the existing soil; then add topsoil within the bed to raise it to the desired level. Dig this added topsoil into the improved native soil—ideally adding more organic matter at the same time—and let the bed settle for at least 2 months before you plant it. If significant settling occurs, mix more topsoil into the bed.

PROBLEM SOILS

Three soil conditions call for remedial or management measures beyond simple amendment.

ACID OR ALKALINE SOIL. Garden soil may be acid, neutral, or alkaline. Soils with a pH (short for potential hydrogen) number less than 7 are acid; those with pH 7 are neutral, while those with a pH above 7 are alkaline. Though roses grow well in soils ranging from moderately acid to somewhat alkaline, extreme cases cause problems: certain nutrients become chemically unavailable to roots, and growth suffers. One important pH-related problem is iron-deficiency chlorosis, found in alkaline soils where iron, even if present, is tied up in insoluble compounds.

In general, alkaline soils are found in low-rainfall, dry-summer regions, while acid types are associated with high rainfall and humid summers. If you suspect that your soil is strongly acid or alkaline, have it tested. The soil test kits sold at nurseries and garden centers will give you a ballpark reading—enough to indicate a potential problem. Professional tests (look in the Yellow Pages under "Soil Laboratories") give more precise readings; some even measure nutrient content and amount of organic matter. In some states, agricultural extensions can run soil tests and suggest remedies for extreme pH imbalances.

COMPACTED SOIL. Soil around new homes is sometimes severely compacted from the heavy equipment used in construction; quantities of building debris also may be hidden beneath the surface. In a non-clay soil, you may be able to solve the problem with deep digging, debris removal, and the addition of organic matter. In the case of compacted clay, though, it may be simpler and less costly to plant your roses in raised beds (see facing page).

SHALLOW SOIL. Sometimes a surface layer of good soil is underlain by a layer of impermeable soil that blocks both roots and water. This situation may arise at new homesites where fresh soil has been spread over soil compacted during construction. The condition also occurs naturally: in low-rainfall regions, a dense hardpan layer often lurks under the surface, and some areas have naturally shallow soil with bedrock close to the surface.

Where the layer of compacted or hardpan soil is fairly thin and the soil beneath it is permeable, you may be able to break through the hardpan and—with considerable effort—remove it from the planting area. More often, though, raised beds offer the simplest means of achieving a planting area with enough depth for good root growth.

---

large pore spaces and acts as a sponge, slowing the passage of water and dissolved nutrients.

In poorly drained soil, organic matter is most useful only when worked into the overall planting area. If you amend just the soil in the planting hole, you'll create a small basin of soil that absorbs water more quickly than the surrounding soil can take it in; the result will be waterlogged soil in the plant's immediate root area. If your soil is fast draining, however, you can amend either the total planting area or just the backfill soil returned to the planting hole. Don't ignore amendments entirely, though; even in well-drained soil, it's beneficial to slow the passage of water and dissolved nutrients at least in the immediate zone around the roots.

To amend a planting area, begin by digging or tilling the soil, ideally to a depth of 1 foot or more. Then spread a layer of organic matter several inches deep over the surface and dig or till it in until thoroughly blended. Water the amended soil and let it settle for at least a week before you plant.

To amend backfill soil, simply mix the soil removed from the planting hole with organic material—up to half each native soil and organic matter, if the soil is fairly sandy. Set the rose in place, then fill in around it with the improved soil.

WHEN TO PREPARE

If you know several months in advance that you're going to plant roses, you can do your preparation early enough to give the soil a good chance to mellow and settle before planting. This is also the time to add phosphorus and potassium fertilizers (see page 107). For autumn planting, prepare the soil in summer; for winter or spring planting, prepare it in early to midautumn.

Amending the soil a few months before planting also lets you safely use fresh animal manures and undecomposed organic materials as improvements, since they'll have plenty of time to break down. These two amendments should not be used at planting time. Fresh manures can burn roots, and undecomposed materials will take nitrogen from the soil to further their decay.

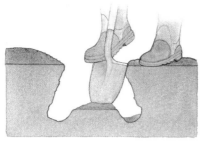

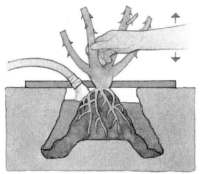

TOP: To plant any rose, start by digging a hole with sides that slope outward from top to bottom; the sides should be rough, not smoothly sculpted. Leave a "plateau" of undug soil at center bottom of hole to help prevent settling; dig edges deeper to facilitate root penetration into soil.

MIDDLE: To plant a bare-root rose, form a firm cone of soil over plateau at bottom of hole, then spread plant's roots over cone; place a stick across hole to gauge proper planting depth (see "How to Plant," at right). Fill in with soil and water well.

BOTTOM: To plant a container-grown rose, loosen soil on surface of root ball and uncoil any circling or twisted roots. Set root ball on soil plateau and spread out loosened roots; add soil beneath root ball, if needed, to adjust planting depth. Fill in with soil and water well.

WHEN TO PLANT

You can plant roses during much of the year. Bare-root plants are sold for dormant-season planting; container-grown plants extend planting time through spring and summer.

Dug from the growing fields in late autumn, *bare-root roses* can go into the ground at any time during the dormant season when soil is not frozen. In much of the South, Southwest, and West Coast—wherever winter lows seldom dip below 10°F/−12°C—January and February are the prime bare-root planting months. In parts of the country where subfreezing temperatures alternate with warm spells and freezing weather can last for several months, late autumn and early spring are the best bare-root planting times. In decidedly cold-winter regions, spring planting is best; if roses are set out in late autumn, they'll produce little or no root growth during winter, and even well-protected plants may be lost during severe cold snaps.

Retail nurseries and garden centers sell bare-root plants at the right planting time for your area, and mail-order nurseries also endeavor to send plants at that time. Whenever you bring plants home or receive them by mail, check them for damage and cut back any broken roots or canes to just below the breaks with sharp pruning shears.

Occasionally, plants shipped during winter will freeze in transit: cells in the canes rupture, and the roots turn black. Overheating in transit also can occur, leaving roots alive but canes black. In both cases, the plants will grow poorly (if at all). Whenever you receive such damaged merchandise, contact the supplier at once. Reputable sources often replace damaged plants, even if the injury was beyond their control.

During the growing season, *container-grown roses* are sold in retail nurseries and garden centers, though they're typically more limited in quantity and variety than bare-root roses. Some mail-order suppliers also ship own-root roses growing in pots of various sizes. The best planting time for any container-grown rose is spring, before temperatures begin to rise; this gives roots a chance to become established before summer heat arrives. Plants set out in hot weather need constant attention to watering to keep their unestablished root systems moist and prevent foliage from wilting.

HOW TO PLANT

When you're ready to set a rose out in the garden, follow the steps shown at left. Proper planting depth depends on whether the rose is budded or on its own roots.

On *budded roses* (see page 99), the bud union is a critical point, since it gives rise to the strongest growth of the rose you want. Exposed to air and sunlight, it tends to produce more canes than it would if buried under an inch or two of soil—but in cold-winter climates, an exposed bud union, even when well protected (see page 116), is more vulnerable to freezes than one snuggled beneath the ground.

In regions where winter lows are not likely to fall below 10°F/−12°C, roses are planted with the bud union at or slightly above soil level. In colder-winter areas, there is no clear consensus. Many growers position the bud union just above soil level, then protect plants heavily over winter or employ "Minnesota tip" protection (see page 117); the feeling is that the occasional loss of a rose over an unusually hard winter is offset by the more robust cane production. Some rosarians, however (especially those in the northern U.S. and southern Canada who use traditional soil-mound protection), position bud unions 1 or even 2 inches below the soil. This is a better guarantee of survival, and some plants will send out roots from above the bud union as well.

With *own-root roses,* planting depth is less of an issue. Where winters are mild, position the juncture of roots and canes even with or just slightly below soil level. In cold-winter areas, place the juncture about an inch below the soil; even if the plant freezes to the ground, new growth springing from the roots will be the rose you want.

GROWING ROSES IN CONTAINERS

Roses will flourish in containers anywhere in the country. That's good news for anyone who wants to enjoy a blooming rose in a pretty pot—but it's especially cheering for apartment and condominium dwellers, who lack the ground for a rose garden. Container growing simplifies winter protection, too: where winter cold is unkind to roses, you simply move the plant to the shelter of a porch, garage, or basement for as long as the subfreezing weather lasts.

CONTAINER CHOICES

Miniature roses thrive in containers as small as the equivalent of a 2-gallon nursery can. But regular-size bushes, standard roses, and climbers need capacious containers to allow well-developed root systems for healthy plants. If you're handy with tools, you can fashion wooden containers of any size, shape, and design. But if you prefer to shop for manufactured containers, go for size. Pots with the soil volume of a 5-gallon nursery can are the smallest ones you should buy, and bigger ones are better. Wooden half-barrels offer a generous volume, and their diameter allows room for seasonal annuals beneath the rose. If you choose unglazed terra-cotta pots, keep in mind that they're porous; plants in these containers need the closest attention to watering. Containers of glazed terra-cotta, wood, concrete, and plastic are more moisture retentive.

Once it's filled with soil and plant, any large container will be heavy. If you'll be moving the container from place to place, consider attaching casters to it or putting it on a platform with casters (make sure the platform has drainage holes that align with those in the container).

Miniature roses are ideal container subjects.

PLANTING AND CARE

Roses in containers need a well-drained, noncompacting soil medium. Packaged planting mixes fit that description, but because they are essentially inert (nutrient-free) media, plants growing in them need frequent fertilizing. You also can fashion your own planting mixes, using organic material for porosity and garden soil to provide a reservoir of some nutrients. If your topsoil tends toward the clay side, use no more than 1 part soil to 3 parts organic matter; if your topsoil is sandy, you can use up to half each topsoil and organic matter.

If you're planting a bare-root rose, position it in the container with the bud union at soil level, or (for own-root plants) with the junction of roots and canes at or just below soil level. If the roots are a bit too long to fit the container, bend them slightly to fit; if they are so long you must coil them to fit, cut them back just enough to eliminate the coiling. If you're planting a container-grown rose, loosen the root ball as shown on the facing page, then position the plant as just instructed for bare-root roses.

Firm the soil around the roots of the newly planted rose, then water well; the soil surface should be about 2 inches below the container rim. If the soil settles too much, grasp the plant just above the roots and, while soil is saturated, jiggle it upward to the proper depth. Then fill in with more soil.

Water plants often enough to keep soil moist (but not soggy). For best performance, fertilize regularly; liquid and timed-release types are the simplest to use (see page 108).

Roses growing in containers do best if their roots are kept cool. To this end, use large containers (so soil heats more slowly), water frequently, and choose a spot where the pot is shaded but the rose is not. In hot-summer regions, both rose and container will appreciate light shade during the afternoon.

Decorative terra-cotta container showcases shrub rose 'Bonica' (page 59).

WATERING

Established rose plants are tough enough to survive on skimpy watering. But mere survival doesn't produce a garden display. To turn in the performance most of us want, roses need moisture in the root zone throughout the growing season. In setting up a watering regime for your roses, you'll need to address three questions. First, how much water do the plants need? Second, how often must you supply it? And finally, exactly how will you provide it?

HOW MUCH AND HOW OFTEN?

An oft-repeated statement is that roses need the equivalent of 1 inch of rainfall each week. In many situations, this may be a conservative estimate. A rose plant needs water to the full depth of its roots (assume 16 to 18 inches), in enough quantity to keep soil constantly moist but not waterlogged. This is accomplished by periodic deep watering, with the interval between waterings depending on soil type, frequency of rainfall, wind, and several other factors.

Soil type determines how much water you'll need to apply with each watering. Clay soils, with their myriad tiny pore spaces, absorb water slowly but hold more of it than do sandy soils, which have fewer but larger pore spaces. Studies performed at the University of California have revealed that 1 cubic inch of water applied to the soil surface penetrates directly downward 1 foot in sandy soil, 6 to 10 inches in loam (intermediate between sand and clay), and 4 to 5 inches in clay. As it relates to watering roses, this means that wetting the soil to a 2-foot depth in a 2-foot-square basin requires 5 gallons of water in sandy soil, 7.6 gallons in loam, and 13.2 gallons in clay.

To determine how deeply a given amount of water penetrates your garden soil, conduct a simple test. Do your normal watering (or a limited-time watering of, say, 30 minutes). The next day, dig a narrow hole 1½ feet deep to see how far the moisture has penetrated. If you discover, for example, that 30 minutes of watering moistened only the top 10 inches of soil, you'll know that longer watering is needed to moisten the entire root zone.

Once you know how *much* water to apply with each watering, you'll need to determine how *often* to water. Again, soil type plays a role here. Sandy soil absorbs water rapidly and needs the least for deep penetration, but it dries out quickly; clay absorbs water slowly and needs a much greater amount for penetration through the entire root zone, but it retains moisture significantly longer. Thus, during "average" spring weather, you may need to water roses growing in sandy soil every 5 days, those in loam every 7 to 10 days, and those in clay every other week.

Several other factors also affect watering frequency. Rainfall and mulches (see "Mulching to Conserve Water," facing page) may let you stretch between-watering intervals by providing or conserving moisture, respectively. Wind, high temperatures, and full sun accelerate transpiration, depleting moisture rapidly and calling for more frequent watering.

The simplest way to determine if it's time to water is to check the soil. Just dig a small hole with a trowel. If the soil is moist at a depth of 3 inches, there's no need to water; if it isn't moist, water again for the time required for adequate penetration. Where spring and summer rain is common, don't assume that rainfall will furnish all the water roses need; check the soil to be sure, and set up a rain gauge to monitor rainfall amounts.

Even in the dormant period, when plants are seemingly inactive, don't overlook watering. As long as the soil is not frozen, continue to water your roses as needed.

HOW TO APPLY WATER

Overhead sprinkling and flood irrigation are the traditional watering methods. Drip irrigation is a more recent introduction, offering a variety of ways to provide water at or near ground level. In summer-rainfall areas, most rose growers choose some form of irrigation; rain may be adequate for cleansing foliage, but it may not be sufficient to penetrate deeply. Where summers are dry, the preferred regime usually is some form of irrigation supplemented by periodic sprinkling to wash the leaves. Wherever there's dust or air pollution, leaves benefit from overhead watering every week or so, both to remove dust and to wash away some insect pests, especially aphids and spider mites.

SPRINKLING. If you want to give your roses overhead water, you can use hose-end sprinklers or install a permanent sprinkler system. You'll find numerous options, among them lawn-type heads that deliver full-circle to fraction-of-a-circle coverage, rotating impact sprinklers that cover a great area from one head, and oscillating kinds that send a rainfall-like spray high and wide. To study your choices, visit a hardware, home improvement, or irrigation supply store. In considering the various permanent types for a possible system in your garden, you'll need to know the pressure of your water supply and its delivery capacity at that pressure. Once you have that knowledge, you'll be able to determine how many of any type of sprinkler you can run at one time and still achieve good coverage.

FLOOD IRRIGATION. Watering by flood irrigation allows for deep penetration without the evaporative loss inherent in sprinkling. It's the clear choice in hot and dry regions, and especially in windy areas.

The simplest way to irrigate roses is to create watering basins. Around each bush, build an earthen dike 2 to 6 inches high and about 3 feet across; then flood the basins and let the water soak into the soil. Adjust the water flow to the soil's absorption rate so the basin won't overflow, then leave water turned on for the time needed for adequate penetration. One occasional objection to basins is that they make roses look as though each is sprouting from its own personal volcanic crater. This problem is easily solved, though: spread a mulch within each basin and between plants as well.

Creative gardeners can design interconnected basins to water many roses at one time—if the soil is level. In some arid areas, growers surround an entire (level) bed with a berm or even a concrete curb to contain irrigation water.

MULCHING TO CONSERVE WATER

In nature, plants are almost always mulched: spent leaves, blossoms, seedpods, and even dead twigs and branches accumulate on the soil beneath and between plants. This natural mulch serves several purposes. It keeps soil cool and moist, by preventing sun from reaching the surface and by imposing a barrier to evaporation; it furnishes a small and ongoing supply of nutrients as it decomposes; and, as it decays and itself becomes part of the soil, it improves soil texture and permeability.

This list of pluses makes it clear that mulching your roses is a good idea. In the garden, one further benefit is weed suppression: a fairly thick layer of mulch effectively prevents existing weed seeds from germinating by blocking out the light they need, and any weeds that sprout within the mulch are easily pulled.

Suitable mulches are many and varied. Compost is available to anyone with the time and space to make it. Pine needles work well, as do the tougher leaves from hardwood trees (oak leaves, for instance; maple and other thin leaves tend to stick together in sheets). With careful management, you can use lawn clippings: spread them in a thin layer and let them dry, then apply another thin layer, and so on. Packaged materials include various wood by-products and animal manures. Regional agriculture furnishes a variety of by-products, including crushed sugar cane residue, cotton burr compost, rice hulls, apple and grape pomace (the residue left after crushing the fruit for juice), ground corn cobs, and many more.

In choosing and using a mulch, keep in mind that high-cellulose mulches (most wood by-products and corn cobs, for example) need nitrogen for their decomposition and will draw it from the soil at the roses' expense. If you use these materials, lightly sprinkle a high-nitrogen fertilizer over the soil surface to offset the nitrogen used in the mulch's decay.

When you apply a mulch, spread it evenly over the soil surface in a layer 2 to 3 inches thick; extend it to within about an inch of each plant's base. (In cold-winter regions, postpone mulching until soil has warmed; spread too soon, a mulch will delay warming and slow growth.)

Pine needle mulch looks attractive, and it's easy for water to penetrate.

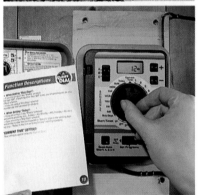

TOP: Soaker hoses deliver water to a rose bed. Mulch of bark chips obscures tubing but doesn't interfere with water delivery.

BOTTOM: An electronic controller can be programmed to activate a watering system automatically, according to a schedule selected by the gardener..

DRIP IRRIGATION. Simply described, drip irrigation concentrates water delivery in a plant's immediate root zone, using special slow-delivery emitters that let you water a great number of plants at one time. Compared to traditional flood irrigation, drip irrigation takes longer to achieve the needed penetration. The foundation of the system is flexible polyethylene tubing about ½ inch in diameter; special plastic fittings let you make normal pipe fitting–type connections. The low-volume emitters can be attached directly to the main tubing or positioned at some length from it, connected by ⅛-inch microtubing ("spaghetti tubing"). Emitters range from actual drip and trickle devices to microsprayers and minisprinklers; delivery rates vary from 1½ to over 20 gallons per hour.

If you prefer to bypass the need for fittings and emitters, you can base your system on soaker hoses (shown at left) or drip tubing. Water simply oozes through this sort of tubing all along its length, either directly through the tubing's walls (in the case of soaker hoses) or through laser-drilled holes (drip tubing). A good filter between water source and tubing is essential, since water delivery will be seriously compromised if pores or holes become clogged.

For any drip irrigation system, you'll find supplies in most hardware and home improvement stores that have garden departments—and, of course, in irrigation supply shops. The system can be linked to your main water line (after you connect an antisiphon device and pressure regulator) or simply attached to a hose or hose bibb. You can arrange the tubing to water an entire bed of roses or lay it out to deliver water to widely separated bushes simultaneously; you also can set up inconspicuous systems that will water all the pots in an extensive container garden. Where winter temperatures fall low enough to freeze water in the tubing, be sure to drain the system in autumn after its final use for the year.

CONTROLLERS

If your planting is served by any sort of permanent or semipermanent water delivery system, you can arrange to water it automatically with an electronic controller (popularly called a "timer"). These devices can be programmed for various watering intervals and durations, letting you water your roses even when you're away. Most controllers operate on standard 110-volt household electricity, though you can buy battery-powered models that will function far from a convenient electrical supply.

Drip irrigation components include a variety of drip emitters, microsprayers, and tubing. An in-line filter attaches to the glossy black ½-inch tube.

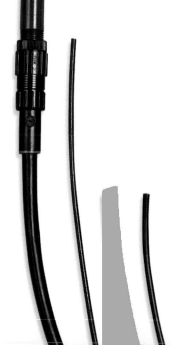

FERTILIZING

A rose that isn't fertilized won't dwindle away. In fact, many species and shrub roses actually flourish without supplemental nutrients. But virtually all modern roses and many of the old garden sorts need at least a little fertilizer during the growing season to turn in their peak performance.

To apply dry fertilizer, scatter it over soil beneath branch spread of rose bush. Lightly scratch it into soil; then apply water to dissolve.

NUTRIENTS IN FERTILIZERS

Nitrogen, phosphorus, and potassium are the *major nutrients*, the three elements used most by plants. *Secondary nutrients* include calcium, magnesium, and sulfur; *trace elements* include zinc, copper, boron, and a number of other elements needed only in minute amounts.

Nitrogen is the most critical element for good growth and bloom. It's also the one major nutrient that is water soluble. This trait means that it can be effectively applied at the soil surface, but it also means that it's rapidly depleted, carried out of the root zone by watering and rain. Nitrogen is furnished by nature, but not in amounts great enough to spur roses on to their lavish best, so you'll need to supplement the natural supply each year.

The other two primary nutrients—phosphorus and potassium—are essentially insoluble, so applying them to the soil surface is of little benefit to plants. To be effective, these elements must be worked into the soil within the expected root zone, an operation best carried out when you prepare a bed for planting.

The secondary nutrients and trace elements also are insoluble (or soluble only to a limited extent). Most soils contain all these in adequate supply for good rose growth, though there are exceptions; sulfur deficiency may occur in high-rainfall areas of the Pacific Northwest, for example. For information on any possible deficiencies in your local soil, contact the nearest Cooperative Extension Agency; if problems exist, you'll be told how to correct them.

TYPES OF FERTILIZERS

In terms of composition, fertilizers are either dry or liquid; in derivation, they are either inorganic (manufactured) or organic (processed from formerly living or naturally occurring materials). The particular choice you make will depend on how convenient you find the product to use and, perhaps, on your philosophy.

Whether dry or liquid, organic or inorganic, all fertilizers can be classed as *complete*—containing all three of the major nutrients (see "Nutrients in Fertilizers," above)—or *incomplete*.

DRY FERTILIZERS. These granular products constitute the bulk of fertilizers sold. Dry organic sorts include blood meal, bone meal, and cottonseed meal; inorganic products cover a vast array of packaged types, from single-element kinds such as ammonium sulfate (containing nitrogen alone) to a range of complete fertilizers, among them the various formulations sold as "rose food."

Controlled-release (timed-release) fertilizers are a special category of dry fertilizers. Pellets of dry fertilizer are coated with a permeable resin; with each watering, a small amount of the fertilizer dissolves and leaches through the coating into the soil. The period of effectiveness depends on the brand: some products release nutrients over a 3- to 4-month period, while others last several months longer.

LIQUID FERTILIZERS. These are liquid or dry concentrates which must be diluted or dissolved in water before application. The nutrients are then absorbed quickly by plant roots, and you'll see results in a short time. An extensive choice of brands and formulas is available; most kinds are inorganic, though organic types (fish emulsion is an example) are also sold.

WHEN AND HOW TO APPLY

The following guidelines apply to roses growing in the ground which have been established for one year or more. Refrain from using dry fertilizers on newly planted roses until their second year in your garden; you can, however, use liquid fertilizer during midsummer of their first year, if you wish. For container-grown roses, liquid and controlled-release types are best.

Positioned between lengths of hose, siphon device extracts liquid fertilizer solution from pail, letting you fertilize plants as you water them.

FERTILIZING SCHEDULES. Soon after you finish pruning, fertilize all roses to give them a nutrient boost for putting out new growth when the growing season begins. Do a follow-up application after the first round of spring bloom has finished. For the exclusively spring-flowering roses, this will be the last application of the year. For repeat-flowering roses, though, continue to apply fertilizer after each subsequent major bloom period; this will work out to approximately every 6 weeks. (This timing applies to dry fertilizers; if you use a liquid type, your applications will need to be more frequent, since the nutrients will leach through the soil more quickly. Apply liquid fertilizers every 3 to 4 weeks, as long as roses are in bloom.)

Keep in mind that dry fertilizers vary in the time lag between application to the soil and availability of nitrogen—the nutrient of most concern—to the plant. For immediate availability, nitrogen must be in its *nitrate* form. If it's applied in other forms, it must be converted to nitrate in the soil before your roses can assimilate it—but its effect tends to be more sustained than that of nitrate, an advantage in the eyes of many gardeners. The availability of nitrogen applied in the *ammonium* form is slightly delayed; slowest to act are the organic and synthetic organic nitrogen forms, such as blood meal, urea, and IBDU (isobutylidene diurea).

Remember that soil type affects nutrient retention. Clay holds dissolved nutrients longest, so fertilizer applied to this type of soil will have the most sustained effect. In sandy soils, you may want to fertilize more often to compensate for faster leaching of nutrients.

In regions where winter temperatures dip below 10°F/−12°C, it's important to stop fertilizing well before cold weather sets in, so the plants won't be loaded with succulent, frost-tender growth when the first freeze hits. A good rule of thumb is to make the last application no later than 6 weeks before the expected first-frost date—anywhere from August 1 to early September, depending on your region.

APPLYING FERTILIZERS. Whatever fertilizer type you use, apply it only to well-watered soil. Fertilizer applied to dry soil and then watered in may burn the surface feeder roots that absorb it.

To apply *dry fertilizer,* lightly scratch the soil surface (no more than 1½ inches deep) beneath the plant; this light cultivation should extend *at least* as far as the branch spread, but keep it several inches away from the base of the plant. Scatter the recommended amount of fertilizer (check the package label) over the cultivated soil; then water well.

For application of *liquid fertilizer* to individual plants, mix the fertilizer in a watering can and apply the recommended amount to each bush. For larger plantings, you may find it more convenient to use an injector device that lets you run the fertilizer solution through your watering system. The simplest of these is a siphon attachment that draws a measured amount of fertilizer into your hose or water line from liquid concentrate in a pail. Another sort is a small canister that attaches between hose bibb and hose (or drip irrigation line); concentrated, soluble powder or tablets in the canister dissolve at a measured rate when water flows through and into the hose or water line.

Foliar fertilizing with liquids is also an option. Because rose leaves can assimilate nutrients, you can supplement soil fertilization with foliar applications; simply spray the nutrient solution onto the leaf undersides, where it is absorbed for almost immediate use. You can use any liquid fertilizer recommended for foliage application (check the label). To help the spray adhere to foliage, add a spreader-sticker to the solution; or use a phosphate-free household detergent, at the rate of ¼ teaspoon to each gallon of solution. A consistent schedule reaps the most benefits. Start in spring when the first leaves have completely formed, then continue to make applications every 2 to 3 weeks—until midsummer in cold-winter regions, until about mid-September where winter is mild. Since foliar fertilizer can burn leaves in hot weather, don't use it when temperatures will reach 90°F/32°C or above.

PESTS AND DISEASES

Roses are no more susceptible to pests and diseases than many other flowering shrubs. Those who raise roses for exhibition may go to great lengths to maintain antiseptic rose beds, since they need blemish-free flowers and foliage—but most gardeners can live quite happily with the occasional nibbled leaf or spotted petal. In the average home garden, the goal is simply to keep potential problems at acceptable, nonepidemic levels.

COMMON-SENSE PEST MANAGEMENT

The first step in keeping pests and diseases in check lies in establishing good plant health.

ATTEND TO YOUR ROSES' BASIC NEEDS, as outlined in this chapter. No amount of any control will turn a sickly rose into a thriving one if, besides pest or disease attack, the plant has to endure poor soil, insufficient water, lack of nutrients, or an unsuitable location.

START THE YEAR WITH A GARDEN CLEANUP. Right after pruning, clear all leaves and other debris (including old mulch) from beneath the bushes; before new growth emerges, spray plants and soil to kill any insect eggs and disease spores. Lime sulfur (calcium polysulfide) or a combination of lime sulfur and dormant oil are traditional dormant-season cleanup sprays; both must be applied before new growth begins. You can also safely use a combination insecticide-fungicide, either during dormancy or after the growing season has begun.

DEAL WITH PROBLEMS AS THEY ARISE. Throughout the year, check your roses frequently, always remembering that your aim is to curtail problems, not eliminate them. Learn the life cycles of the pests and diseases that may afflict your planting, and realize that there's no point in attempting control before they appear or in continuing it after they naturally depart. (For foliage diseases, though, preventive treatment is justified.)

If pest damage becomes unacceptable and you must take action, be guided by the following pointers:

Try the least toxic control first (see list on page 110) if you have the choice. Some pests can be dislodged from foliage with a forceful spray of water. Less toxic alternatives carry the advantage of being less harmful to beneficial insects—an important consideration, since pests' natural enemies can aid you in your management campaign.

Repeat control measures as needed. A single application of a nontoxic agent or contact spray usually won't accomplish long-term control. A follow-up treatment, generally within 7 to 10 days, is needed to catch any insects that hatch (or any disease spores that germinate) after the initial round.

Read instructions on spray labels carefully and follow them to the letter. If you're tempted to deviate from the directions, always seek advice from your Cooperative Extension agent, a reputable nursery, or a successful local rose grower.

Consider combining sprays to address more than one problem at one time. Many synthetic insecticides and fungicides can be mixed; some pesticides are also compatible with liquid fertilizers, letting you include foliar feeding in a pest-control program. Before mixing, however, always check product labels for compatibility information or warnings; if you can find no such information, *don't* mix.

SPRAYERS AND SPRAYING

Even if you use only nontoxic controls, you'll probably need some sort of spray applicator. The one that's best for you will likely be dictated by the size of your garden. A small plot may be easily covered by a 1-gallon model, but large areas call for a more capacious sprayer.

For just a few plants, hose-end sprayers are convenient, though they do have a few drawbacks. These devices consist of a bottle (in which you mix spray concentrate) and a siphon which attaches to it; the unit then attaches to your hose. The concentrate is measured into the flow of water from the hose and sprayed out through a nozzle. Because hose-end sprayers discharge a greater amount of spray material than other types do, they are much more wasteful when used over a large area (and more hazardous, too, if you're using toxic material). These sprayers also make it more difficult to spray undersides of leaves.

MOSAIC VIRUS

Leaves displaying a yellow zigzag pattern are a telltale sign of mosaic virus. This systemic infection is transmitted and perpetuated through the budding process. An infected understock transfers the virus to the rose variety budded onto it; budwood taken from an infected variety produces more infected plants. The virus is not transmitted by pruning shears or insects. Aside from being unsightly, mosaic virus is debilitating; it reduces overall vigor and decreases flower production. Because there is no cure, you cannot treat infected plants; you can either live with the disfigured foliage or discard the plant and try to replace it with virus-free stock.

The most efficient, easiest-to-use sprayers are compressed-air tank types. They're available in several styles. The most widely used kind features a cylindrical tank with an attached flexible hose that ends in a metal tube and, finally, a nozzle. You measure the spray concentrate into the tank and dilute it with water, then close the tank top and pump a plunger to propel the solution through the hose and out the nozzle. The nozzle is at about a 45-degree angle to the metal tube, making it easy to spray the undersides of leaves. Tanks vary in volume from 1 to 6 gallons; if you opt for one of the larger ones, you may want to consider a wheel attachment that will let you roll it through the garden.

The backpack-type tank sprayer, typically with a capacity of about 4 gallons, eliminates the roll-versus-carry question. The tank straps comfortably on your back; you hold the hose and spray nozzle with one hand and use the other to work a pump handle to maintain pressure. Gasoline-powered models are available that maintain constant pressure.

Some dedicated growers with large rose collections appreciate the efficiency of a wheel-mounted gas or electric tank sprayer that operates at maintained pressure and throws a forceful, finely atomized spray over a considerable area. These are sold in capacities ranging from about 10 to over 100 gallons.

TIPS FOR SPRAY APPLICATION. Whether you use a nontoxic agent or a chemical product, proper application is important.

Begin by watering roses thoroughly a day before spraying; this reduces the risk of foliage being burned by the control agent. Pay attention to timing: spray when the air is still, generally in the early morning (after dew has evaporated) or early evening. As you spray, thoroughly cover both sides of leaves. Start at the base of each bush and spray the leaf undersides, working upward with a side-to-side rolling movement of the nozzle; by the time you reach the top, the "rainback" dripping from sprayed leaves will have covered much of the upper surfaces.

If you use chemical controls, protect your skin with rubber gloves, a long-sleeved shirt, and long pants. Wear goggles to protect your eyes and a mask to guard against inhaling mist or fumes. When using a wettable-powder pesticide (a dry product expressly designed to be applied in solution), first dissolve it thoroughly in a little hot water; then add this solution to the spray container for further dilution.

With any control, be mindful of spray drift. Chemical agents (and even some nontoxic ones) can kill beneficial insects inhabiting nearby plants. Many chemicals are lethal to wildlife, especially fish and honeybees. When using such sprays, cover fish ponds and birdbaths; never discard excess spray or wash spray equipment where the runoff could enter ponds or streams.

Once the job is done, *do not* save leftover spray for later application; it may lose its potency, and it can pose a hazard. Mix fresh solution for each round of spraying. To keep your sprayer in good condition and prolong its life, clean it thoroughly after each use.

PLANT PROBLEMS AND REMEDIES

The chart on the facing page shows the pests and diseases most likely to afflict roses and recommends a range of controls for each. The remedies fall into four categories, listed below in order of increasing toxicity.

HAND MEANS. You pick off or squash pests, or wash them off with water. No sprays of any kind are used.

NONTOXIC. Though they are not synthetic poisons, these are lethal to the target pest. They include baking soda, horticultural oil, insecticidal soap, lime sulfur, pyrethrum products, and the biological control *Bt (Bacillus thuringiensis)*.

CONTACT CHEMICAL. These synthetic toxic chemicals kill the organism by surface contact. Included are abamectin, carbaryl, chlorothalonil, copper compounds, diazinon, dicofol, fluvalinate, malathion, maneb, mancozeb, zineb.

SYSTEMIC CHEMICAL. The toxic ingredient is absorbed into the plant; for a period of time after application, the offending organism is killed as it takes in the plant's juices. These include acephate, dimethoate, fenarimol, triforine.

| Aphids | Beetles (Japanese) | Black spot | Cane borers | Caterpillars | Crown gall |
| Downy mildew | Mites | Powdery mildew | Rose midges | Rust | Thrips |

PROBLEM	DESCRIPTION	CONTROLS
Aphids	These soft-bodied, ⅛-inch-long insects may be green, red, brown, or black. They appear on new growth, especially in early spring; if present in great numbers, they can slow growth and stunt or deform leaves. Natural enemies (ladybugs in particular) help control them.	Hose off with water; spray with insecticidal soap, pyrethrum products, diazinon, malathion.
Beetles	Various beetles may visit roses. Many do little damage and are easily hand-picked. Japanese beetles are troublesome in eastern North America; check with Cooperative Extension agent for best control.	Hand-pick; spray with carbaryl, diazinon, malathion.
Black spot	Circular black spots with irregular, fringed edges appear on leaves (most conspicuously) and stems; tissue around spots may turn yellow. This fungal disease thrives in warmth and is spread by water (rainfall, sprinklers); if unchecked, it can defoliate a plant. Spores overwinter in cane lesions and possibly on old leaves.	Spray with combination of baking soda and horticultural oil (2 tsp. of each per gallon of water), chlorothalonil, fenarimol, triforine.
Cane borers	These worms bore into new shoots and consume the stem's pith; the sudden collapse and wilt of new growth tips is a clear indication of infestation. Hand-picking is the only sure remedy.	Hand-pick by cutting off infected stems and crushing them.
Caterpillars and worms	Collectively, this group includes various wormlike pests (larvae of flying insects) that skeletonize or chew holes in leaves. Extent and severity of damage determine the need for control.	Hand-pick; spray with *Bt,* carbaryl, diazinon, fluvalinate.
Crown gall	Bacterial infection produces rounded, lumpy, tumorlike galls—usually at a plant's base, but they can appear on roots and, in advanced cases, on canes. Infected plants decline and eventually die.	Cut away galled tissue; leave cut surfaces exposed to sunlight and air for several days. Dig and discard badly infected plants.
Downy mildew	This fungal disease produces purplish red leaf spots with irregular, smudged outlines; leaves turn yellow and drop. Canes can also become infected. Disease is spread in water, overwinters in cane lesions and on old leaves. Temperatures above 80°F/27°C kill spores.	Spray with fungicide containing copper, manganese (maneb, mancozeb), or zinc (zineb).
Mites	These tiny spider relatives suck juices from surface tissue, causing yellowed, dry-looking leaves that, in heavy infestations, show silvery webbing on their undersides. Hot, dry weather favors mites: the higher the temperature, the more eggs are laid and the the more rapidly the pests mature. Give repeat treatments to control emerging generations.	Hose off with water; spray with horticultural oil (summer weight), abamectin, diazinon, dicofol.
Powdery mildew	Fungal disease produces gray to white, furry to powdery coating on new growth of leaves, stems, flower buds. Leaves become crumpled and distorted, and remain so after fungus is killed. Disease needs dry leaves to establish, but flourishes in humid conditions; it is encouraged by crowding (with accompanying poor air circulation), shade, fog.	Spray with combination of baking soda and horticultural oil (2 tsp. of each per gallon of water), triforine.
Rose midges	Near-microscopic winged insects (about ½₅ inch long) rasp tender tips of new growth, causing it to shrivel and blacken. Because the larvae pupate in soil, soil treatment is the most effective control.	Treat soil with diazinon (spray with liquid solution or apply granules).
Rust	Small orange spots on leaf undersides enlarge to form thick, powdery masses of orange spores; yellow blotches appear on leaf surfaces. Disease starts in late spring; severe infection can defoliate a plant.	Spray with chlorothalonil, triforine.
Thrips	These nearly invisible insects deform and discolor flower petals by rasping and puncturing tissues—starting in buds, where they work among unopened petals. White and pastel flowers are their favorites.	Spray with diazinon, acephate, dimethoate.

Pruning

You prune a rose to promote a symmetrical bush, encourage new growth, and remove dead, damaged, or diseased wood. These are simple objectives, yet many novices are daunted by the prospect of pruning. Over the years, both low ("hard") and high ("light") pruning have been promoted as the way to do it. Today, an understanding of plant physiology and rose ancestry coupled with trial-and-error data has led to the view that light to moderate pruning (when you have that option) produces the best possible garden plants and plenty of good-quality flowers.

Pruning shears with bypass (scissor-action) blades make the cleanest cuts. Hold them with the cutting blade lowermost, the hook above.

A good pruning cut slants at approximately a 45-degree angle. Its lowest point is opposite and slightly higher than the growth bud on the stem; the upper point is ⅛ to ¼ inch directly above the bud.

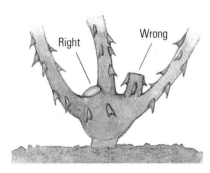

When removing an entire cane, cut it flush with the bud union or growth from which it sprang. If you leave a stub, it will die back into the union, allowing entry for disease.

HOW A ROSE GROWS

A rose's roots, stems, and leaves work together to encourage growth and productivity. The roots absorb nutrients, which are then transported upward and throughout the stems in specialized cells. At the same time, leaves absorb carbon dioxide from the atmosphere, then convert it into sugars and other nutrients which are carried throughout the plant in other specialized cells.

Not all absorbed nutrients and synthesized substances (such as sugars and proteins) are used immediately; some are stored in the tissues of roots and stems for use at other times of the year. Proteins, for example, are stockpiled in wood and bark cells toward the end of the growing season, then used by the plant in early spring (before leaves mature) to manufacture compounds needed for renewed growth.

Many roses have smooth green bark on young, vigorous growth (1), while bark on older canes becomes grayed and scaly. When older canes produce only spindly new growth (2), they should be completely removed at pruning time. Some roses have new growth that is bronzed to purple (3) or mottled green (4); even their year-old—and still productive—canes may be gray and scaly. Cut back to these strong stems; remove canes entirely only when they fail to produce strong new growth.

Because roses store so much potential energy in their canes, hard pruning imposes hardships. When you prune away much stem growth, you discard resources stored for starting spring growth, thus forcing the plant to rely on the reserves in its roots for the initial growth push. Because the root system enlarges in proportion to the size of the plant, continued heavy pruning results in a small root system with correspondingly small amounts of stored nutrients. Heavily pruned plants produce less overall growth at first flush than do lightly or moderately pruned ones, and they therefore have fewer leaves available to synthesize nutrients for new growth.

TIMING AND TOOLS

For repeat-flowering roses, the best time to prune is toward the end of the dormant season, when growth buds along the canes begin to swell. In mild-winter regions, this can be as early as January; in the coldest-winter areas, April may offer the first opportunity. In the many areas where chilly, wintry days alternate with more springlike spells during March and April, gardeners often use one of two indicators to determine pruning time: they either prune when forsythia comes into bloom, or they prune 30 days before the area's last expected killing frost (Cooperative Extension agents can furnish this data).

To prune roses well, you need sharp pruning shears and a small pruning saw. The shears handle most of the work, but a pruning saw's narrow blade is needed for removing larger-diameter canes and those in areas too awkward or congested for shears to reach.

PRUNING HYBRID TEA, GRANDIFLORA, AND FLORIBUNDA ROSES

Regardless of where you live, you can apply the following guidelines to pruning these widely grown modern roses.

Remove unproductive wood. Cut out all dead wood and weak, twiggy branches. If an older cane produced only weak growth, remove it entirely.

Open up the bush. Remove branches that cross through the center. This gives you a vase-shaped plant—slender or fat, depending on the plant's natural habit—without a central tangle of twigs and leaves that can harbor insects and diseases. (*Note:* Rather than removing these central branches, growers in very hot climates often just shorten them, so they will produce leaves to shade the canes.)

Cut back remaining stems. In mild-winter regions, remove up to one-third the length of all new growth formed during the past year. In cold-winter regions, where canes may be killed back to their protection, you will have to cut back more heavily. Leave as much healthy, live wood as you can, but remove all wood damaged or killed by winter cold. Cut back stems until you encounter healthy white pith.

Cut to outward-facing buds. This reduces the amount of new growth that will grow into the plant's center. Bushes with a very spreading habit are an exception: on these, cutting to inside buds can encourage more upright growth.

Cover pruning cuts. Wherever cane borers (see page 111) are a serious problem, seal all pruning cuts you have made into pencil-thick or larger stems. A simple sealant is ordinary white glue, the sort sold in a plastic squeeze bottle with a dispenser top.

Remove sucker growth on budded plants. Grasp the sucker cane and *pull* it down and off the plant. Simply cutting it off won't solve the problem; you'll be left with undeveloped growth buds at the sucker's base, which will produce more suckers in years to come.

PRUNING A HYBRID TEA, GRANDIFLORA, OR FLORIBUNDA

Ready for pruning, a dormant bush will be leafless or nearly so. You will see many stems and twigs of varying thicknesses, ages, and health.

Entirely remove old canes that produced no strong growth during the last year, branches that cross through bush's center, and twiggy, weak stems. Shorten growth that remains (see next 2 drawings).

In mild-winter regions, after you remove unproductive and superfluous growth, reduce length of remaining healthy stems by about one-third.

In cold-winter regions, remove unproductive growth and cut back all dead and damaged stems after you remove protection; final size depends on the severity of the past winter.

STANDARD ROSES

A standard rose (popularly known as a "tree rose") is a three-piece plant. The root system is provided by one of the usual understock roses used in the production of budded bush roses (see page 99). Budded onto the understock is a rose that will produce a straight, strong cane—the trunk of the standard-to-be. When the trunk is a year old, the desired rose variety is budded onto it at a specific height, forming the standard's head.

The trunk is a standard rose's most vulnerable part; if it breaks, you've lost the variety you wanted. At planting time, give a standard a sturdy stake; place it on the sunny side of the trunk to ward off possible sun scald, and let it extend into the head to increase stability.

In pruning a standard, the accent is on symmetry. Follow the general guidelines given for hybrid teas on page 113; after pruning, the head should have a more or less dome-shaped outline.

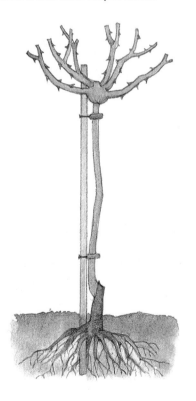

PRUNING MINIATURE ROSES

The pruning approach used for hybrid teas works for miniatures as well. Cut out dead wood and spindly stems, and remove canes that produced only weak, twiggy growth during the year. This will leave you with a vase-shaped to rounded plant consisting of healthy, vigorous stems. Reduce this growth by about half, pruning to outward-facing growth buds; the finished plant should have a symmetrical outline.

PRUNING SHRUB AND OLD GARDEN ROSES

The growth habits of these roses vary from shrubby to nearly climbing. Some, in fact, produce long, arching canes that can be trained in the manner of climbers; these should be pruned as directed for spring-flowering or repeat-flowering climbers (below), whichever applies. Most of the roses in these groups, however, are vigorous plants that need a bit of annual shaping and thinning but relatively little cutting back. Since most are grown as specimen shrubs, pruning is aimed at maintaining a shapely silhouette that fits well into the landscape. Remove all dead growth; cut out old canes and weak ones that are not producing strong new growth. Finally, shape the bush, if necessary, by cutting back wayward stems that skew the overall symmetry.

Repeat-blooming shrubs should be pruned at the same time as hybrid teas: in late winter or early spring, just before new growth begins.

Spring-flowering shrubs are traditionally pruned right after flowering has finished; strong new growth made after bloom will bear flowers the following spring. Many rose growers, however, find it simpler to do some pruning during the dormant, leafless period, when it's easier to see all growth and to remove the pruned stems. At that time, you can cut out dead and old, unproductive stems, as well as canes that would bear few flowers in spring. A touch-up pruning after the flowering season has ended will finish the year's pruning work.

PRUNING SPECIES ROSES

Most of these roses flower only in spring and correspond to spring-blooming climbers or shrubs, depending on their growth habit. Prune as directed for spring-flowering climbers and spring-flowering shrub roses. For repeat-blooming kinds, prune as directed for repeat-flowering shrub roses.

PRUNING CLIMBING ROSES

A variety of roses climb: true climbers, climbing sports of bush roses, and some shrub types that can get carried away in mild climates. What all of these have in common is long, variably flexible canes that produce most of their flowers from growth buds along their lengths.

REPEAT-FLOWERING CLIMBERS. In this group are the most widely planted climbing roses: natural climbers (ranging from large-flowered to miniature) and climbing sports of hybrid teas, grandifloras, floribundas, miniatures, and several old garden rose classes.

When you plant one of these roses, let it grow unpruned for 2 to 3 years; this gives it time to become established and build up strength to put out good climbing canes. During that time, simply remove dead wood, weak growth, and spent flowers. Tie new canes into position as they mature (see "How to Train Climbing Roses," page 74). After this settling-in period, the plant will consist solely of long canes produced in your garden; these will produce flower-bearing side branches (laterals). Climbing varieties differ in how they produce canes: some tend to send up a few new ones from the ground each year, while others build up a more permanent woody structure and produce most long new growth from higher on the plant.

In pruning these climbers, you want to encourage growth of flower-bearing laterals and stimulate production of new canes that will replace the older ones as they become less productive. Each year, just before growth begins, prune out only the old and obviously unproductive wood—that is, stems that produced no strong growth the previous year. Next, cut back to two or three buds all of the laterals that bore flowers during the last year. Avoid cutting back vigorous new, long canes unless space compels you to do so; always try to train them into place first.

SPRING-FLOWERING CLIMBERS. Pruning at the start of the growing season cuts away some of that spring's potential flowers. For the most abundant bloom, therefore, delay pruning these roses until just after flowering. However, just as is true for the other exclusively spring-flowering roses, the dormant period before growth starts may be the easiest time to remove dead and unproductive wood. At either time, cut out old canes and stems that have produced only weak growth and few flowers, then thin out the less vigorous of any tangled stems that remain. After blooming, the plant will put out new canes and laterals to carry next spring's flowers. On spring-blooming climbers, you won't accomplish much by removing spent flower clusters: some varieties may produce secondary blooms from the midst of old flower clusters or just below them, and many develop a crop of decorative hips.

RAMBLERS. Included here are hybrids primarily of *Rosa wichuraiana*, though a few other species (*R. multiflora*, *R. setigera*, and *R. sempervirens* in particular) have produced offspring that fit into this category. In late spring, these climbers cover themselves with clusters of small blossoms; after bloom, they send out long, limber canes from ground level and a lesser number of long laterals from growth that has flowered. The next spring's bloom comes on this new growth.

Prune these ramblers after flowering has finished and when new growth has started. Completely remove canes that have just flowered and show no sign of producing any long, vigorous new shoots. On canes that have flowered and are starting to send out some strong new growth, cut back only to this new growth. As the new canes and laterals lengthen and mature, train them into position.

REGULATING GROWTH DURING THE YEAR

After your roses have put on an inch or two of new growth in spring, check over the emerging new shoots to see what direction they're taking. Break or rub out any that are poorly located or unnecessary (crossing through the center of the bush, for example). Sometimes two or three new shoots will grow from one leaf axil; carefully break out all but the strongest one.

It's a good idea to remove spent blossoms from the modern repeat-flowering roses—hybrid teas, grandifloras, floribundas, miniatures, and climbers. This keeps plants looking neat and thwarts seed-setting, which occurs at the expense of flowering. Cut stems as far down as necessary to keep the bush shapely, cutting above an outward-facing growth bud above a five-leaflet leaf (buds above three-leaflet leaves produce weaker stems). During and after the first bloom flush, refrain from cutting long stems. In this early part of the season, plants have fewer leaves to manufacture nutrients; the more leaves they retain, the more growth will be encouraged. Wait to cut long stems until mid- to late summer, when bushes are full of foliage and have leaves to spare. You can deadhead repeat-flowering shrub roses as well, though their general vigor usually keeps them productive without this attention.

Newly planted roses, as well as weak or small plants you're trying to build up, need all the leaves they have to manufacture nutrients. Just snap off the faded flowers and leave all the foliage; refrain from cutting blossoms with stems for indoor decoration.

PEGGING CANES FOR MORE BLOOM

Between stiff bushes and limber climbers are a number of species roses, old garden types, and shrub roses with an arching or fountainlike habit ('Ulrich Brunner fils', page 39, and 'Complicata', page 61, are two examples). Like true climbers, these can be encouraged to produce more flowering laterals by the 19th-century process of pegging. Bend canes outward into broad arcs, then tie their tips to stakes (pegs) driven into the ground. Where plants are intertwined or space is limited, you can bend and arch the young stems, then tie them to stiffer older canes to hold them in place.

Use length of twine to tie end of flexible rose cane to sturdy stake (TOP). Where staking is impractical, arch over stems and tie them to older, stiffer canes (BOTTOM).

Blanket of insulating snow covers rose garden bedded down for the winter.

WINTER PROTECTION

In milder regions, all roses are safe from the risk of winter freeze damage. In much of the country, however, providing cold protection is part of routine rose-garden maintenance.

Generally speaking, modern hybrid teas, grandifloras, miniatures, and climbers run little risk of damage in areas where winter lows seldom dip below 10°F/−12°C. Some floribundas and many shrub and old garden roses can remain unprotected where 0°F/−18°C is a standard low temperature, and a few species and species hybrids are even tougher. Occasional temperatures colder than the stated minimums may or may not hurt exposed canes, but prolonged episodes are sure to be damaging.

TIPS FOR WINTER SURVIVAL

Winter protection is designed to keep plants consistently cold, not warm: the objective is to hold thoroughly dormant canes at a fairly constant temperature within a range of 15° to 25°F/−9° to −4°C. Sudden, rapid, or frequent changes in temperature present a serious hazard. Because moisture in the canes expands as it freezes, quick freezing breaks cell walls inside the canes and destroys plant tissue; repeated bouts of freezing, thawing, and refreezing can ruin exposed canes.

Besides constructing artificial protection for your rose bushes (see facing page), you can minimize the effect of winter cold on your plantings in other ways. First, remember that location and exposure influence the intensity of cold and the extent of temperature fluctuation. Cold air sinks, so valley gardens are colder than those on surrounding hillsides, and the lowest parts of your garden are the coldest ones. Roses planted in such low spots obviously run the greatest danger of freezing and should be well insulated; they are also the most vulnerable to damage by late freezes.

Second, be aware of the effects of wind. Cold wind dries out canes: the rose's roots cannot take up water from frozen soil to replace that evaporated by wind, and the result is desiccated canes that may die or fail to produce vigorous growth. Moreover, winter wind is often distinctly colder than still air—the "wind chill factor" mentioned by meteorologists. Gardens sheltered by walls or by plantings that serve as windbreaks are likely to be warmer than exposed gardens. If climbing roses are planted against a wall that provides shelter and raises temperatures by means of reflected heat, they may be able to survive in regions slightly beyond their normal hardiness limit.

Third, be sure to provide good care during the growing season. Plants maintained in vigorous good health throughout the year—not defoliated by disease or insects—are better equipped to survive winter than are weaklings. It's also important to adjust care so the roses are "mature," not still actively growing and blooming, when the first frosts arrive: because of its higher water-to-starch ratio, immature new growth is more vulnerable to freezing than mature growth. About 6 weeks before the expected first-frost date, withhold nitrogen fertilizers to lessen production of new growth. Leave all September blossoms to wither naturally on the plants, since any hips they form will help bring the entire plant to a well-ripened state, ready to face several months of cold.

PREPARATION AND PROTECTION

Though protection methods vary, some basic steps are common to all. Begin with a thorough cleanup: clear away all old leaves and spent flowers, and remove all debris and mulch from around each plant's base. Next, strip away and discard any leaves remaining on the canes. This sort of sanitation helps prevent future insect and disease problems by eliminating places where eggs and spores could overwinter. Whether you intend to protect plants by mounding alone or by mounding plus open-topped cylinders (see illustrations on facing page), cut canes of each bush back to about 3 feet and tie them together to keep them from whipping about in wind.

Don't rush to protect plants too soon. You can mound their bases in early to midautumn, but wait until the soil freezes to apply mulch over the mounds. Just before you expect soil to freeze, give the roses a deep soaking; if roots are well watered, the plants can better resist the desiccating effects of wind.

For "Minnesota tip" protection (illustrated on facing page), bury plants when they are well matured but before soil freezes. In the really cold-winter areas where this method is most useful, midautumn is an average target time. As for mounded plants, cut canes of each bush back to about 3 feet and tie them together before burial.

REMOVING PROTECTION

In early spring, weather can be unpredictable. Any number of times before springtime truly settles in, you may experience sudden shifts from warm temperatures to freezes and back again. For this reason, resist the urge to remove protection at the first breath of spring. In general, the best time to remove it is the time best for dormant-season pruning in your area.

WINTER PROTECTION METHODS

Cut canes back to a manageable height and tie them together, then mound soil at least 1 foot high over base of bush. After soil mound freezes, cover it with an insulating mound of straw, hay, cut conifer boughs, or other noncompacting organic material. For greater security, surround insulated bush with a wire mesh cylinder: this will hold soil mound and its covering in place while allowing water to drain away easily.

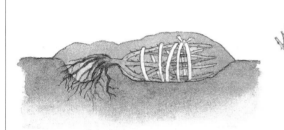

"Minnesota tip" protection involves loosening roots on one side of a plant, bending it over into a trench on the opposite side, and then covering everything—roots and plant—with soil.

To "tip" a standard, loosen roots on side opposite bud union of understock and trunk, then bend plant over bud union into trench; pin trunk into place, then cover with soil.

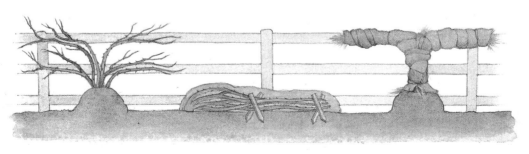

Where winter lows range from 5° to 15°F/−15° to −9°C, protect nonhardy climbing roses with soil mounds (left). Where lows will drop below −10°F/−23°C, remove climbing canes from supports and cover them with soil (center). Where low temperatures fall in the 5° to −10°F/−15° to −23°C range, you can leave climbing canes in place if you insulate them with straw, then cover the insulated canes with burlap.

PROPAGATION

With so many roses available for sale, why bother starting your own? Simple pleasure is the usual reason: imagine being able to point out a beautiful rose that you nurtured from just a scrap of wood! There are practical reasons, too. Starting your own plants is the only way to get plants of unidentified roses and of varieties no longer sold. And if you need many plants of a particular rose, home propagation is a thrifty decision. Gardeners with a creative urge (and a bit of the gambler's spirit) may want to try raising entirely new roses from seed.

NEW PLANTS FROM CUTTINGS

You can start cuttings at almost any time of year. Use softwood during the blooming season; use dormant (hardwood) stems in autumn, winter, or early spring, depending on climate.

SOFTWOOD CUTTINGS. Follow the steps described and illustrated on the facing page, starting with a stem that has just flowered. At top end of stem, cut just above a leaf; at bottom end, cut beneath a leaf, then remove lowest leaves.

Once the potted cuttings are covered with plastic bags (as shown), place them in a shaded but well-lit spot where they will be warm but not overheated. Rooting should occur within 1 to 2 months; during this time, cuttings should not need watering. To test for rooting, gently pull on a cutting; if you feel resistance, roots are forming. When new growth shows that cuttings have rooted, gradually remove bags. Start by opening bag tops a bit to let new growth begin adjusting to reduced humidity. After a few days, open tops completely; if new growth remains firm, remove bags entirely. Keep new plants lightly shaded while they adjust to the open air; water often enough to keep new growth from wilting. If you like, you can transfer these rooted cuttings to individual pots of lightweight potting soil, but be sure to keep roots moist during the transplanting process. By the next planting season, they should be ready for setting out in the garden.

HARDWOOD CUTTINGS. Make 8-inch-long cuttings of pencil-thick stems; the base of the cutting should be a straight cut just below a growth bud, while the top should be a slanting cut just above a bud. Remove the two lowest growth buds, then dip the base end in rooting hormone. You can plant cuttings in pots or in the ground. For pot culture, insert cuttings 3 to 4 inches deep in pots (such as 1- or 2-gallon nursery containers) filled with a light, sandy potting mix. For in-ground planting, dig a trench and spread about an inch of coarse sand in the bottom; then set in cuttings, upright and 3 to 4 inches deep, and fill in around them with a mixture of half sand, half soil. By the end of the first flowering flush in spring, you should be able to see which cuttings have rooted. By the next planting season, they'll be ready for transplanting to the garden.

NEW PLANTS BY BUDDING

Most bare-root rose bushes sold each winter are budded plants propagated by the method illustrated below. Commercial grow-

NEW PLANTS BY BUDDING

1 Make a 1-inch-long T-shaped cut in bark of understock, an inch or two above soil level.

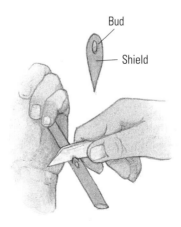

2 For budwood, choose a stem that has just flowered. Slice beneath bud (starting from above it) to get 1-inch shield of bark containing growth bud.

3 Peel back understock bark at T cut; insert bud shield (trim lower end if needed for fit). Bud should finish at least ¼ inch below top of T.

ers use understock roses that root easily, accept most roses budded onto them, produce well-balanced root systems, and are easily dug and shipped. The two most popular commercial understocks are *Rosa multiflora* (see page 18) and 'Dr. Huey', a maroon red, semidouble climber that flowers only in spring. 'Dr. Huey' is preferred in mild-winter regions; *R. multiflora* does better with at least a little chill, though it succeeds almost everywhere. For at-home budding, either of these two works well; the simplest way to get them is from sucker growth on budded plants you've purchased. Besides these choices, you can use almost any vigorous, easy-to-root rose (climbers provide the most wood). Old ramblers such as 'American Pillar' (see page 76) and 'Dorothy Perkins' (see page 78) have been used, and the Noisette-alba hybrid 'Mme. Plantier' (see page 66) once had a small career as a commercial understock. In mild-winter regions, you might try any of the *R. banksiae* forms (see page 16) or *R. × fortuneana*.

Prepare and root understock cuttings as described for hardwood cuttings on facing page and at right, but gouge out all but the top two growth buds to eliminate the potential for sucker growth below the bud. The budding process is simplified if you root cuttings in pots; you can then work at table height rather than at ground level.

Budding is best done in spring and summer, with the earlier time applying to milder-winter regions. The understock must be sufficiently succulent that its bark peels back easily from the stem to accept the bud.

For successful budding, you need to make absolutely clean cuts, and this means using a razor-sharp knife. You can buy special budding knives; some come with flattened handles designed to lift the bark flaps formed by the T cut. To tie the bud in place, you can use a variety of items. Plastic plant-tie tape is widely available, sold in nurseries and in hardware and home improvement stores with garden departments. Horticultural supply houses sell budding rubber (5- to 8-inch strips like wide rubber bands) as well as the easiest-to-use option: plastic bud patches that completely cover a bud and clip together on the opposite side of the understock stem.

Success or failure will show in about 3 weeks after budding. If the bud is still plump and green, you have a success. If the bud is brown and shriveled, try inserting another bud on the same understock, a bit lower down and on the opposite side.

SOFTWOOD CUTTINGS

Start with 8-inch stems that have just flowered. Dip bottom ends of stems in rooting hormone, stick cuttings in pot of perlite, and water well. Insert a stake in pot, then enclose pot in a plastic bag (stake in pot keeps bag upright).

HARDWOOD CUTTINGS

Start with pencil-thick 8-inch cuttings of previous season's growth. Gouge out two lowest growth buds, then dip bottom ends of cuttings in rooting hormone. Plant cuttings directly in ground or insert them in pots filled with lightweight potting mix; water well.

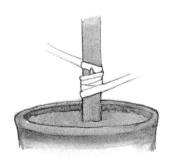

4 Firmly tie bud in place with plastic or rubber strip, wrapping both above and below it but leaving bud exposed. Remove tie when you're sure of success.

5 When bud sends out a strong new shoot, or the following spring (whichever comes first), cut off understock growth about 1 inch above the shoot or bud.

Bud at left is at stage to be prepared to receive pollen. Remove petals and cut away all stamens, leaving just stigmas to receive pollen (center). Cover with paper bag to prevent contamination. Open flower (right) shows anthers at stage where they shed yellow pollen grains. When stigmas of prepared bud are sticky (a few hours to a day after you prepare bud), apply pollen to them; then replace bag for a week.

By late summer, hips will have formed; these contain rose seeds, as shown in cut-open hip in center.

Plant seeds in sterile, lightweight potting mix, spacing them 1 to 2 inches apart.

NEW PLANTS FROM SEED

Professional rose breeders produce new varieties by hybridizing one rose with the pollen of another, then growing plants from the resulting seeds. Home growers can find hybridizing an engaging pastime as well, though it's important to bear in mind that most seedling plants will not measure up to their parents.

To get the knack of harvesting, planting, and growing seedlings, you may want to plant seeds from the hips that form on roses in your garden. Until the mid-19th century, most new roses came from such naturally occurring crosses. Once you find how simple and intriguing the process is, you'll be eager to try making hybrid crosses of your own.

CROSSING AND HARVESTING. In mild-winter regions, you can make crosses (as shown at left) in spring and summer; where frosts come in October, do all hybridizing with the first crop of bloom in spring. The rose hips will take about 4 months to develop to the harvesting stage; they're ripe and ready to pick when they turn red, orange, yellow, or brown.

Germination is generally more successful if you give hips an after-ripening period of low (but not freezing) temperatures in a moist atmosphere. To do this, just enclose the ripe hips in plastic bags, cover them with damp peat moss, vermiculite, or sand, and place them in the vegetable crisper of your refrigerator. After 6 to 8 weeks, the hips will be black and partially decomposed. At this point, take them from the bags and remove the seeds; these will be of odd sizes and shapes, and not all will be viable. To test for viability, put the seeds in water; those that sink are capable of germination, those that float are not.

PLANTING THE SEEDS. Plant seeds ⅜ to ½ inch deep in lightweight, sterile potting mix. You can plant closely in shallow containers, then transplant the seedlings to larger containers or small individual pots when they have their first set of true leaves; or you can plant seeds about 2 inches apart in deeper (at least 3-inch-deep) pots and let them flower without transplanting. Germination may start within 6 weeks of planting and continue for about 2 months; some seeds that fail to germinate during this period may do so in the next year. You can expect seedlings of bush hybrid teas, grandifloras, floribundas, and miniatures to flower as soon as 6 weeks after germination. Climbing roses and some shrub and old garden roses may not bloom for 2 to 3 years.

GROWING THE SEEDLINGS. In mild-winter regions, you can plant seeds and raise seedlings entirely outdoors.

In colder areas, an indoor start—in a greenhouse, on a sunny windowsill, or under artificial light—is the best approach. This lets seedlings begin to grow well before outdoor roses do; they'll bloom before the garden comes into flower, then have the full growing season to develop outdoors. Carry the potted seedlings outside as soon as the danger of frost is past; protect them from wind and direct sunlight for about a week, until they adjust to the outdoor atmosphere. After a year's growth outdoors, those you want to keep for further observation will be ready to plant in the ground at the next bare-root planting time.

To raise seedlings under artificial lights, use the 40-watt fluorescent tubes made especially for growing indoor plants. A two-tube fixture is satisfactory, but a four-tube setup is preferable, since it gives better light distribution. Position the lights about 6 inches above the containers and leave them on for 16 hours each day.

Damping-off fungi are the main enemy of tiny seedlings, rotting plants at soil level or even before they break the surface. Using clean, sterilized containers filled with a sterile potting medium goes a long way toward eliminating this danger. As a further precaution, you can dust seeds with a powdered fungicide before planting them. Should damping-off develop, water the seedlings with a fungicide solution containing captan.

Freshly picked from the garden, a bucketful of mixed roses awaits final cutting and arranging.

CUT ROSES FOR INDOORS

When your roses are strutting their stuff, it's a shame to leave all the blossoms outdoors. If you cut some of the blooms to display in your home or office, you can enjoy their beauties for the better part of every day.

Once roses have been established for a year or more and are putting out plenty of new growth, cutting some flowers does no harm. Think of it as pre-deadheading! With smaller plants, be conservative: cut just a few flowers with fairly short stems. If plants are large and vigorous, though, you can go for a greater quantity of longer-stemmed beauties.

For the longest-lived bouquets, cut your roses early in the morning or in late afternoon to early evening. If you have the time, immerse the cut stems in water up to the flowers' bases for about an hour before arranging the blooms in a vase; leaves absorb water, and this will enhance freshness.

Always choose a clean vase, since an unwashed container may harbor bacteria which will shorten the flowers' life. Before placing your cut roses in the vase, recut the stems under water, making slanting cuts and leaving as much foliage as possible on each stem. Then recut the stems under water every other day, cutting each back by about an inch.

To further increase your cut roses' longevity, you can add various products to the water in the vase. For best results, anything you add should contain three main ingredients: an acidifying agent; sugar; and an agent to kill organisms that would plug water-conducting cells in the stems. Certain "home remedies" have been used with varying degrees of success; these include aspirin, lemon-lime soda (regular, not diet), chlorine bleach, even copper pennies. Such materials present at least two disadvantages, however: first, none of them has all three of the ingredients noted above; and second, you don't really know the right amount to use. Manufactured floral preservatives are a more reliable choice. They contain the necessary ingredients and include directions telling you just how much to add.

Rosa foetida 'Bicolor'

GLOSSARY OF TERMS

As you read about roses, you're bound to run across certain terms again and again.
Here are a few of the most frequently used words and phrases in the rose-growing world.

AARS. Abbreviation for All-America Rose Selections, Inc. (see facing page).

AoE. Abbreviation for Award of Excellence, given by the American Rose Society to miniature roses that have shown exceptional performance over a 2-year period in test gardens throughout the United States.

BUD. In rose jargon, this word has several meanings. Used as a noun, it refers either to an unopened flower or to the growth bud ("eye") found where leaves join stems. As a verb, it refers to the process of creating new plants by budding (see page 99).

BUD UNION. On a rose that has been propagated by budding (see page 99), the bud union is the point where the desired flowering variety joins the understock. It's an enlarged knoblike area above the roots, from which the plant's canes grow.

CALYX. *See* Sepals.

CANES. The main stems of a rose. They form the plant's framework and grow from or very close to its base.

CODE NAME. New rose varieties are registered with the International Registration Authority for Roses (IRAR). The majority of these are registered under code names, the first three letters of which generally incorporate part of the name of the originator or introducing firm (MAC for McGredy, MEI for Meilland, and so on). Though a rose is officially recognized worldwide by its code name, it is marketed under one or more commercial synonyms which (presumably) have greater appeal. The 1998 AARS winner registered as FRYxotic (FRY for Fryer's Nurseries, Ltd., Cheshire, England), for example, is sold under the more euphonious name 'Sunset Celebration' (page 52).

DOUBLE. In some 19th-century rose literature, a double flower is defined as one containing 10 to 14 petals—about twice the number in a single flower. Today, however, the word "double" describes flowers having 25 or more petals. Very full-petaled flowers are called "very double."

EYE, GROWTH EYE. *See* Bud.

HARDWOOD. Growth that has stiffened and become woody. When you take hardwood cuttings for propagation, you take them from growth of the year just past: hard but still young.

HIP. The seed-bearing fruit formed when a rose is pollinated. Rose hips ripen in autumn, turning a variety of colors, from orange through red to brown.

HYBRID. A seed-grown plant arising from a cross of two genetically different parents. A hybrid may favor one or the other parent (though it is genetically distinct from both); or it may not look like either one.

LATERAL. A secondary stem arising from a growth bud along a main cane.

OLD EUROPEAN ROSES. Rose varieties in classes that developed from European and Eurasian species before the introduction of roses from China in the late 18th century. The old European classes are alba, centifolia, damask, and gallica; the centifolia and damask moss roses are also included here.

OLD GARDEN ROSES. The rose classes developed before 1867, the year the first recognized hybrid tea, 'La France', was introduced. These classes include the old European roses (above) plus those derived at least in part from Asian roses: Bourbons, Chinas, hybrid perpetuals, Noisettes, Portlands, and teas.

OWN-ROOT. An own-root rose is one propagated from a cutting, so that both roots and stems belong to one and the same rose. In contrast to own-root roses are budded ones, in which stem growth and root growth come from two different roses (see page 99).

PEDICEL. The fairly short, leafless stalk that supports an individual flower. A pedicel has no growth buds.

PEGGING. The practice of bending and securing to the ground canes of nonclimbing roses which nonetheless have arching or lax growth. Flowering laterals will grow from buds along the pegged canes.

PILLAR-CLIMBER, PILLAR ROSE. A relatively small, fairly stiff-growing climbing rose that can be trained upright (as on a pillar or post) and still produce flowering laterals from buds along the canes.

PLANT PATENT. A patent, in force for 17 years, that can be issued to the originator or marketer of a new plant. Nearly all new roses are patented. During the patent's lifetime, the patent holder is supposed to receive a small percentage from the sale of each plant—providing some financial support for further research and hybridizing.

QUARTERED. In some exceptionally double roses, the petals are not only packed tightly together in a circular, nearly flat flower; they also appear to be grouped into four more or less equal quadrants. Hence, the blossoms are described as "quartered." Examples include the centifolia 'Paul Ricault' (page 27) and the damask 'Gloire de Guilan' (page 22).

SEMIDOUBLE. This term describes a flower containing roughly between 8 and 20 petals, arranged in more than one layer but still opening to show stamens in the blossom center.

SEPALS. The somewhat leaflike structures that encase the flower bud; in roses, the sepals are green. Collectively, the sepals are referred to as the *calyx*.

SINGLE. This term describes a rose blossom with 5 to 8 petals, arranged in one layer around a central cluster of stamens.

SOFTWOOD. New growth that is flexible and not yet woody. When you take softwood cuttings for propagation, you take them from somewhat flexible growth that is not fully mature; it usually has leaves attached.

SPECIES. A wild-growing plant, often found over a sizable geographic area. All individuals of that plant have virtually the same appearance and genetic makeup, and seeds raised from them will produce more plants virtually identical to the parent.

SPORT. A spontaneous mutation in growth habit or flower character (such as color or doubleness) that occurs on an estab-lished variety; it is most often seen as a branch that differs notice-ably from its parent plant. Plants propagated from the sport reproduce it as a distinct new variety. Typical of a *growth sport* is a climbing form of a bush variety. An example of a *color sport* is 'Chicago Peace' (page 43), with blossoms in a blend of pink and orange-yellow; it was found on a plant of 'Peace' (page 49), which normally bears light yellow and pink flowers.

STAMENS. The male, pollen-bearing parts of a flower. In a rose blossom, they are grouped in the center, around the stigma. Each stamen consists of a threadlike *filament* topped by an *anther* (which contains the pollen).

STANDARD. Often called a "tree rose," a standard is a bush rose budded onto a vertical understock stem which serves as a trunk (see page 114). Sizes vary greatly, from miniature standards on 1- to 1½-foot stems to floribunda and hybrid tea standards on trunks 2 to 3 feet tall. Occasionally you will encounter a 6-foot weeping standard; the head is a lax-caned rambler that cascades to the ground.

STIGMA. The female flower part that receives pollen; it tops the *style*, a stalklike tube rising from the *ovary* (in which seeds will form after pollination). Together, the ovary, style, and stigma make up the *pistil.*

SUCKER. Any growth arising from below the bud union on a budded plant. This growth is that of the understock rose and should be removed (see page 113).

TREE ROSE. *See* Standard.

UNDERSTOCK. The rose that furnishes the root system of plants propagated by budding (see page 99).

ALL-AMERICA ROSE SELECTIONS

In 1938, leading rose growers founded the nonprofit organization All-America Rose Selections, Inc. (AARS), both to establish a test program for new varieties and to publicize those which proved especially worthy. Those few would be designated AARS winners; the first of these appeared in 1940. Today, the AARS testing system operates nationwide, evaluating roses in accredited test gardens throughout the United States. The AARS Test Garden Committee oversees each site, ensuring high standards of culture that are comparable from one garden to the next.

To qualify for an AARS award, a rose must first be entered in the trials. Multiple plants go to each designated test garden, where they are grown for 2 years and evaluated for beauty, distinctiveness, disease resistance, vigor, growth habit, and productivity. When the 2-year test period ends, the winners are determined by tabulating the results of secret-ballot elections held at all the gardens. Plants of the winning rose (or roses) are then shipped to the AARS display gardens (there are currently 137 such gardens), giving the public the chance to admire the victors in the year their awards are announced.

Thanks to the rigorous test system, AARS winners are guaranteed to be vigorous plants that will perform well in a wide range of climates. For this reason, they offer novice growers a good introduction to the joys of rose growing. The absence of an AARS designation, however, does not automatically brand a rose as inferior. First, not all new varieties are entered in the trials—so highly worthy roses can reach the market without AARS testing. Second, some roses, whether entered in AARS trials or not, perform superbly in some climates or regions but are outclassed by other roses elsewhere.

For information, contact All-America Rose Selections, Inc., 221 N. LaSalle St., Suite 3500, Chicago, IL 60601; tel. (312) 372-7090.

Just Joey

A GUIDE TO SELECTING ROSES

Ultimately, choosing the "right" roses is entirely subjective; you pick the ones you like (or think you'll like). Often, though, you'll be looking for specific characteristics—intense fragrance, cold tolerance, a climbing habit. We list 10 such categories below, each with a list of roses that fill the bill especially well.

ROSES FOR HEDGES AND SCREENS

All That Jazz (page 58)
Apothecary's Rose (page 20)
Ballerina (page 59)
Betty Prior (page 59)
Blanc Double de Coubert (page 59)
Bonica (page 59)
Carefree Beauty (page 60)
Carefree Delight (page 60)
Carefree Wonder (page 60)
Champlain (page 60)
Cherry Meidiland (page 61)
Europeana (page 62)
First Light (page 62)
F. J. Grootendorst (page 62)
Frau Dagmar Hartopp (page 63)
Hansa (page 64)
Iceberg (page 64)
Livin' Easy (page 65)
Morden Blush (page 66)
Penelope (page 67)
Pink Grootendorst (page 67)
Pink Meidiland (page 67)
Queen Elizabeth (page 50)
Rosa Mundi (page 21)
Royal Bonica (page 68)
Sally Holmes (page 68)
Showbiz (page 68)
Simplicity (page 69)
Snow Owl (page 69)
The Fairy (page 71)
Trumpeter (page 71)

ROSES FOR GROUND COVERS

Dortmund (page 78)
Flower Carpet (page 62)
Magic Carpet (page 65)
Nozomi (page 91)
Red Cascade (page 91)
Red Ribbons (page 68)

Sea Foam (page 69)
Watermelon Ice (page 71)
White Meidiland (page 71)

TALL CLIMBERS

Aimée Vibert (page 34)
Alberic Barbier (page 75)
Albertine (page 75)
Alister Stella Gray (page 34)
American Pillar (page 76)
Belle Portugaise (page 76)
Bobbie James (page 76)
Cl. Cécile Brunner (page 77)
Cl. Peace (page 77)
Cl. Souvenir de la Malmaison (page 77)
Dorothy Perkins (page 78)
Dr. W. van Fleet (page 78)
Félicité et Perpétue (page 79)
François Juranville (page 79)
Jaune Desprez (page 35)
Lamarque (page 35)
Mermaid (page 80)
Mme. Grégoire Staechelin (page 81)
Paul's Himalayan Musk Rambler (page 82)
Rosa banksiae (page 16)
Rosa laevigata (page 17)

SHORT CLIMBERS

Abraham Darby (page 58)
Alchymist (page 75)
Aloha (page 75)
Altissimo (page 76)
Blaze (page 76)
Cl. First Prize (page 77)
Complicata (page 61)
Cornelia (page 61)
Crépuscule (page 34)
Don Juan (page 78)
Dublin Bay (page 78)
Dynamite (page 78)

Eden (page 78)
Gertrude Jekyll (page 63)
Graham Thomas (page 63)
Handel (page 79)
Henry Kelsey (page 80)
Hugh Dickson (page 38)
John Cabot (page 80)
Joseph's Coat (page 80)
Lavender Lassie (page 65)
Mme. Isaac Pereire (page 33)
Mme. Legras de St. Germain (page 25)
Mme. Plantier (page 66)
New Dawn (page 81)
Othello (page 67)
Paul's Scarlet Climber (page 82)
Piñata (page 82)
Sally Holmes (page 68)
Sombreuil (page 83)
Tour de Malakoff (page 27)
Variegata di Bologna (page 33)
Wenlock (page 71)
William Lobb (page 29)
Zéphirine Drouhin (page 33)

ESPECIALLY COLD-TOLERANT ROSES

Alba roses (pages 24–25)
Blanc Double de Coubert (page 59)
Carefree Beauty (page 60)
Carefree Delight (page 60)
Carefree Wonder (page 60)
Centifolia roses (pages 26–27)
Champlain (page 60)
Damask roses (pages 22–23)
Delicata (page 61)
Dortmund (page 78)
F. J. Grootendorst (page 62)
Frau Dagmar Hartopp (page 63)
Gallica roses (pages 20–21)
Hansa (page 64)
Henry Kelsey (page 80)
John Cabot (page 80)

Martin Frobisher (page 66)
Morden Blush (page 66)
Moss roses (pages 28–29)
Pink Grootendorst (page 67)
Thérèse Bugnet (page 71)
William Baffin (page 83)

SHADE-TOLERANT ROSES

Aimée Vibert (page 34)
Alba roses (pages 24–25)
Alberic Barbier (page 75)
Altissimo (page 76)
Awakening (page 76)
Betty Prior (page 59)
Cornelia (page 61)
Félicité et Perpétue (page 79)
Golden Showers (page 79)
Kathleen (page 65)
Mermaid (page 80)
Mme. Grégoire Staechelin (page 81)
New Dawn (page 81)
Paul's Scarlet Climber (page 82)
Rosa moschata (page 17)
Sally Holmes (page 68)
The Fairy (page 71)

THORNLESS (OR NEARLY THORNLESS) ROSES

Aimée Vibert (page 34)
Belle de Crécy (page 20)
Chloris (page 25)
La Belle Sultane (page 21)
Mme. Legras de St. Germain (page 25)
Paul Neyron (page 39)
Rosa banksiae, double forms (page 16)
Ulrich Brunner fils (page 39)
Veilchenblau (page 83)
Zéphirine Drouhin (page 33)

ROSES WITH SHOWY AUTUMN HIPS

Alba Semi-Plena (page 24)
Ballerina (page 59)
Blanc Double de Coubert
  (page 59)
Carefree Beauty (page 60)
Cherry Meidiland (page 61)
Dortmund (page 78)
Frau Dagmar Hartopp (page 63)
Hansa (page 64)
Kathleen (page 65)
Mme. Grégoire Staechelin (page 81)
Penelope (page 67)
Rosa canina (page 16)
Rosa eglanteria (page 16)
Rosa glauca (page 17)
Rosa moschata (page 17)
Rosa moyesii (page 18)
Rosa multiflora (page 18)
Rosa rugosa (page 19)
Rosa virginiana (page 19)

NOTABLY FRAGRANT ROSES

Abraham Darby (page 58)
America (page 76)
American Beauty (page 38)
Angel Face (pages 58, 77)
Arlene Francis (page 42)
Belle Story (page 59)
Blanc Double de Coubert (page 59)
Centifolia roses (pages 26–27)
Camelot (page 43)
Chrysler Imperial (page 43)
Cl. Étoile de Hollande (page 77)
Constance Spry (page 77)
Damask roses (pages 22–23)
Dolly Parton (page 44)
Double Delight (page 44)
Fair Bianca (page 62)
Fragrant Cloud (page 45)
Fragrant Memory (page 45)
French Perfume (page 45)
Gallica roses (pages 20–21)
Général Jacqueminot (page 38)
Hansa (page 64)
Heirloom (page 45)
Henry Nevard (page 38)
Intrigue (page 64)
John F. Kennedy (page 46)
Just Joey (page 46)
King's Ransom (page 46)
La France (pages 46, 72)
Lamarque (page 35)

Maréchal Niel (page 35)
Margaret Merrill (page 65)
Medallion (page 47)
Mirandy (page 47)
Mister Lincoln (page 48)
Mme. Isaac Pereire (page 33)
Moon Shadow (page 48)
Oklahoma (page 48)
Othello (page 67)
Perfume Delight (page 50)
Pink Peace (page 50)
Portland roses (page 32)
Prince Camille de Rohan
  (page 39)
Proud Land (page 50)
Radiant (page 91)
Scentimental (page 69)
Secret (page 51)
Souvenir du Docteur Jamain
  (page 39)
Stainless Steel (page 52)
Sterling Silver (page 52)
Sunsprite (page 70)
Sweet Chariot (page 90)
Sweet Surrender (page 52)
Tamora (page 70)
The Squire (page 71)
Tiffany (page 53)
Ulrich Brunner fils (page 39)
Wenlock (page 71)
White Dawn (page 83)

SINGLE FLOWERS

Altissimo (page 76)
Anemone (page 76)
Ballerina (page 59)
Betty Prior (page 59)
Carefree Delight (page 60)
Cherry Meidiland (page 61)
Complicata (page 61)
Dainty Bess (page 44)
Dortmund (page 78)
Flutterbye (page 63)
Frau Dagmar Hartopp
  (page 63)
Kathleen (page 65)
Mermaid (page 80)
Mutabilis (page 31)
Nearly Wild (page 67)
Nozomi (page 91)
Pink Meidiland (page 67)
Playboy (page 67)
Sally Holmes (page 68)
Sparrieshoop (page 70)
Species roses, most (pages 16–19)

ROSE SOCIETIES

Most rose growers enjoy sharing their experiences with other enthusiasts, and rose societies offer a perfect forum for participating in the camaraderie of rosemania.

THE AMERICAN ROSE SOCIETY
P. O. Box 30,000
Shreveport, LA 71130
(318) 938-5402

Founded in 1899, the ARS provides its members with 11 monthly magazines and one magazine-format annual. Members also receive an annual booklet giving point-score ratings—derived from surveys of ARS members—for all roses currently grown in the United States. Two national conventions are held each year. Of special interest to novice rose growers is the ARS's Consulting Rosarian Program, a nationwide network of experienced growers offering advice on the varieties and cultural methods best for your region.

THE CANADIAN ROSE SOCIETY
c/o Anne Graber
10 Fairfax Crescent
Scarborough, Ont. M1L 1Z8
Canada

Established in 1913, the CRS sends its members three journals and a softcover annual each year; meetings and other activities are held at the regional and national levels. Gardeners in cold-winter parts of the northern United States will find helpful advice on varieties and cultural techniques.

HERITAGE ROSES GROUP
Beverly R. Dobson, Secretary
1034 Taylor Ave.
Alameda, CA 94501

Devotees of old roses formed the HRG in 1975. A quarterly *Heritage Roses Letter* goes out to all members; six districts, each headed by a regional coordinator, offer regional contact through gatherings and publications.

Mary Rose

Golden Showers

Mail-order Rose Suppliers

When you go rose shopping, you'll find that mail-order suppliers offer the widest assortment of roses in all classes. For the ultimate shopping guide, you might want to invest in the Combined Rose List. Updated annually, this booklet provides an index of all roses commercially available from growers in the United States and Canada, as well as those in Great Britain, continental Europe, and other overseas locations. For current CRL prices, contact Peter Schneider, P. O. Box 677, Mantua, OH 44255 (via e-mail: PeterSchneider@compuserve.com).

MODERN ROSES

EDMUNDS' ROSES
6235 Southwest Kahle Rd.
Wilsonville, OR 97070
(503) 682-1476

JACKSON & PERKINS CO.
One Rose Land
Medford, OR 97501
(800) 292-4769

TATE ROSE NURSERY
10306 FM 2767
Tyler, TX 75708
(903) 593-1020

MODERN AND HISTORIC ROSES

THE ANTIQUE ROSE EMPORIUM
9300 Lueckemeyer Rd.
Brenham, TX 77833
(409) 836-9051

ARENA ROSE CO.
536 West Cambridge Ave.
Phoenix, AZ 85003
(602) 266-2223

CORN HILL NURSERY, LTD.
R. R. 5
Petitcodiac, NB E0A 2H0
Canada
(506) 756-3635

HIGH COUNTRY ROSES
P. O. Box 148
Jensen, UT 84035
(800) 552-2082

HEIRLOOM OLD GARDEN ROSES
24062 Riverside Dr. NE
St. Paul, OR 97137
(503) 538-1576

HERITAGE ROSES OF TANGLEWOOD FARMS
16831 Mitchell Creek Dr.
Fort Bragg, CA 95437
(707) 964-3748

HISTORICAL ROSES
1657 West Jackson St.
Painesville, OH 44077
(216) 357-7270

HORTICO, INC.
723 Robson Rd., R. R. 1
Waterdown, Ont. L0R 2H1
Canada
(905) 689-6984;
(905) 689-9323

MARTIN & KRAUS
P. O. Box 12
Carlisle, Ont. L0R 1H0
Canada
(905) 689-0230

MENDOCINO HEIRLOOM ROSES
P. O. Box 670
Mendocino, CA 95460
(707) 877-1888;
(707) 937-0963

PETALUMA ROSE CO.
P. O. Box 750953
Petaluma, CA 94975
(707) 769-8862

PICKERING NURSERIES, INC.
670 Kingston Rd.
Pickering, Ont. L1V 1A6
Canada
(905) 839-2111

REGAN NURSERY
4268 Decoto Rd.
Fremont, CA 94555
(800) 249-4680

ROS-EQUUS
40350 Wilderness Rd.
Branscomb, CA 95417
(707) 984-6959

SEQUOIA NURSERY
See listing under "Miniature Roses"

SPRING VALLEY ROSES
P. O. Box 7
Spring Valley, WI 54767
(715) 778-4481

VINTAGE GARDENS
2833 Old Gravenstein Hwy. South
Sebastopol, CA 95472
(707) 829-2035

WAYSIDE GARDENS
1 Garden Lane
Hodges, SC 29695
(800) 845-1124

MINIATURE ROSES

JUSTICE MINIATURE ROSES
5947 Southwest Kahle Rd.
Wilsonville, OR 97070
(503) 682-2370

MICHIGAN MINIATURE ROSES
45951 Hull Rd.
Belleville, MI 48111
(313) 699-6698

NOR'EAST MINIATURE ROSES
P. O. Box 307
Rowley, MA 01969
(800) 426-6485

OREGON MINIATURE ROSES, INC.
8285 Southwest 185th Ave.
Beaverton, OR 97007
(503) 649-4482

PIXIE TREASURES
4121 Prospect Ave.
Yorba Linda, CA 92686
(714) 993-6780

SEQUOIA NURSERY
2519 East Noble Ave.
Visalia, CA 93292
(209) 732-0190

TEXAS MINI-ROSES
P. O. Box 267
Denton, TX 76202
(817) 566-3034

TINY PETALS NURSERY
489 Minot Ave.
Chula Vista, CA 91910
(619) 422-0385

WEE GEMS MINIATURE ROSES
2197 Stewart Ave.
St. Paul, MN 55116
(612) 699-2694

INDEX

Boldface listings refer to rose classes, culture, and history. *Italic page numbers* refer to photographs.